A Christian We...

SWEET EXCUSES

STOP LYING TO YOURSELF AND START LOSING WEIGHT

TERESA SHIELDS PARKER

Copyright © 2022 Teresa Shields Parker

SWEET EXCUSES
STOP LYING TO YOURSELF AND START LOSING WEIGHT

Printed in the USA
ISBN: 978-0-9861592-5-1
Published by Write the Vision | Columbia, Missouri

All Rights Reserved. This book is protected by the copyright laws of the United States of America. This book may not be copied or reprinted for commercial gain or profit. The use of short quotations is permitted. Permission will be granted upon request. The author guarantees all contents are original and do not infringe upon the legal rights of any other person or work.

Scripture quotations marked NLT are taken from the Holy Bible, New Living Translation, copyright ©1996, 2004, 2015 by Tyndale House Foundation. Used by permission of Tyndale House Publishers, Carol Stream, IL 60188. Used by permission. All rights reserved.
Scripture quotations marked ESV are from The ESV® Bible (The Holy Bible, English Standard Version®), copyright © 2001 by Crossway, a publishing ministry of Good News Publishers. Used by permission. All rights reserved.
Scripture quotations marked KJV are taken from The Authorized King James Version. Rights in the Authorized Version in the United Kingdom are vested in the Crown. Reproduced by permission of the Crown's patentee, Cambridge University Press.
Scripture taken from the Amplified® Bible is marked AMP. Copyright © 1954, 1958, 1962, 1964, 1965, 1987 by The Lockman Foundation. Used by permission.
Scripture taken from the Common English Bible is marked CEB. Copyright © 2011 by the Common English Bible, Nashville, TN. All rights reserved. Used by permission
Scripture taken from The Living Bible is marked TLB. Copyright © 1971 by Tyndale House Foundation. Used by permission of Tyndale House Publishers Inc., Carol Stream, IL 60188. All rights reserved.
Scripture taken from the Contemporary English Version is marked CEV. Copyright © 1995 by American Bible Society. Used by permission.
Scripture taken from The Message ® is marked MSG. Copyright © 1993, 1994, 1995, 1996, 2000, 2001, 2002. Used by permission of NavPress Publishing Group. Colorado Springs, CO. All rights reserved.
Scripture taken from the New American Standard Bible® is marked NASB. Copyright © 1960, 1962, 1963, 1968, 1971, 1972, 1973, 1975, 1977, 1995 by The Lockman Foundation. Used by permission.
Scripture taken from the HOLY BIBLE, NEW INTERNATIONAL VERSION ® is marked NIV. Copyright © 1973, 1978, 1984 Biblica. Used by permission of Zondervan. All rights reserved.
Scripture taken from the New King James Version of the Bible is marked NKJV. Copyright © 1982 by Thomas Nelson, Inc. Used by permission. All rights reserved.
Scripture taken from The Passion Translation® New Testament with Psalms, Proverbs and Song of Solomon is marked TPT. Copyright © 2017 by BroadStreet Publishing® Group, LLC. Used by permission. All rights reserved.
Scripture quotations marked WEY are from the Weymouth New Testament by Richard Francis Weymouth, 1912. Public domain in the United States.

Write
THE VISION.NET
www.TeresaShieldsParker.com

*"Trust God from the
bottom of your heart;
don't try to figure out
everything on your own.*

*"Listen for God's voice in everything
you do, everywhere you go;
He's the one who will
keep you on track.*

*"Don't assume that you know it all.
Run to God! Run from evil!*

*"Your body will glow with health.
Your very bones will
vibrate with life!"*

PROVERBS 3:5-8 MSG

DEDICATION

In Memory of
Lindy Brookhart Stevens

You fought the good fight of faith. There is no one who fought food addiction more boldly and courageously than you. You fought it with God on your side.

In spite of disease and illness you still stood your ground. You shook your fist in the devil's face and told him to get behind you in Jesus' name.

You were a shining light in a world that can be very dark. You were the butterfly waiting to be released and now you are flying across Heaven safe in the Father's arms.

This book is dedicated to your memory because you kept going and overcame your excuses. Now you have laid hold of your reward.

Save me a place at that great fellowship table that includes Jesus and all the saints. I'll meet you there, my sweet friend.

—TERESA SHIELDS PARKER

"Don't copy the behavior and customs of this world, but let God transform you into a new person by changing the way you think. Then you will learn to know God's will for you, which is good and pleasing and perfect."

ROMANS 12:2 NLT

AUTHOR'S NOTE

In May of 2014, God began talking to me about starting an online Christan weight loss coaching group. Even though I had gone through life coaching training and the remarkable freedom coaching training, as well as being ordained by Joan Hunter ministries, getting a master's degree in Biblical studies, and losing over 250 pounds, I didn't feel qualified to coach

When I weighed 430 pounds I had well-meaning people tell me to just eat less and move more. Great plan but when you've programmed yourself to eat away your emotions, it's just not as easy as summoning up the willpower to eat what you know you should. Exercise at 430 pounds, or any time we are overweight, is a foreign word. I was so exhausted from carrying around that extra weight, I couldn't exercise

To climb out of our excuses is mentally exhausting. To sort out the myriad of voices that scream at us is emotionally exhausting. To try to do what we know we should do feels impossible because we have already programmed ourselves to eat a certain way. We live on autopilot until we change our habits.

This book will point out why we believe our excuses to be real, how we can kick them to the curb, and how we can learn to trust God to teach us how to follow Him. He doesn't care what we weigh, but He does care about our health.

Sweet Excuses: Stop Lying to Yourself and Start Losing Weight is a prophetic book. I unknowingly prophesied it into existence eight years ago when God asked me to begin coaching. I told Him I couldn't because, "I know every excuse in the book."

I didn't realize I would one day be writing a book about that very subject. However, it is truer that true that I actually do know and have given God every excuse in this book and many others.

I can now say I not only wrote the book on excuses, but with God's help I gave advice about how to overcome those excuses and trust God for the outcome.

PRAYERS AND QUESTIONS

At the end of each chapter is a heartfelt prayer for you to pray. There are also thought-provoking questions to answer. These can be used for both personal and group studies. These are keys to getting the most out of this book.

The verses that come up again and again are those that have pulled me out of the excuses that almost buried me. I pray they will rescue you as well.

Proverbs 3:5-8 MSG is one of those passages. "Trust God from the bottom of your heart; don't try to figure out everything on your own. Listen for God's voice in everything you do, everywhere you go; He's the one who will keep you on track. Don't assume that you know it all. Run to God! Run from evil! Your body will glow with health, your very bones will vibrate with life!"

I am ready to glow with health and I can't wait for that bones vibrating thing! How about you?

CONTENTS

- 11 ENDORESEMENTS
- 19 CHAPTER 1
  ## EXCUSES, EXCUSE
- 31 CHAPTER 2
  ## PROCRASTINATION IS AN EXCUSE
- 43 CHAPTER 3
  ## I WANT WHAT I WANT
- 55 CHAPTER 4
  ## I'M AFRAID OF FAILURE
- 69 CHAPTER 5
  ## I LOVE A PARTY!
- 83 CHAPTER 6
  ## I CAN'T LOSE WEIGHT
- 97 CHAPTER 7
  ## FEAR OF SUCCESS
- 111 CHAPTER 8
  ## FOOD KEEPS ME SANE
- 127 CHAPTER 9
  ## FOOD WILL PROTECT ME
- 141 CHAPTER 10
  ## FOOD IS MY FRIEND
- 157 CHAPTER 11
  ## DON'T ROCK THE LOVE BOAT

171	CHAPTER 12
	STOP ALL THE NOISE
187	CHAPTER 13
	GOD DOESN'T SPEAK TO ME
201	CHAPTER 14
	DO I HAVE A VOICE?
215	CHAPTER 15
	TOO OLD TO EAT HEALTHY
227	CHAPTER 16
	NO DIET WORKS FOR ME
241	CHAPTER 17
	GOD DOESN'T CARE IF I AM FAT
253	NEXT STEPS

ENDORSEMENTS

SUGAR ADDICTION BROKEN, 50 POUNDS GONE
Denise Mitchell, Avoca, NY

God directed me to Teresa Shields Parker and Overcomers Academy just over two years ago. The transformation in me physically, mentally, and most important, spiritually has been humbling.

The journey I am taking with the Lord, aided by Teresa and the beautiful women involved in the Overcomers group, has been life changing. I have broken my addiction to sugar, stopped binge eating, and lost 50 plus pounds, for good this time!

There is still a work in me to do. I still have some pounds that need to leave my body for optimal health. Overeating is still a struggle as is my willingness to surrender my all to God on a daily basis.

I'm so looking forward to learning even more by way of Teresa's new book, *Sweet Excuses*. I'm ready to dismiss any excuses that arise in my mind, so I can gain total health for this earthly body in order to do His heavenly work here on earth.

MIRACLE IN THE MORNING
Sally Robinson, Red Bluff, CA

A painful night on my knees in heartfelt prayer led me to a miracle in the morning. That miracle was finding Teresa Shields Parker's podcasts and books!

I am so grateful to have begun my own personal journey to reverse the 50 plus years of sugar addiction and emotional eating. Thank you Lord! Thank you, Teresa, for living out your story in such an honest, open way.

LONGINGS FULFILLED
Taryn Gilmore-Cotton, Chicago, IL

I can't lose weight because every time I try, I fail. Besides, I have too much weight to lose anyway, I'm too tired, too busy, don't have time to exercise, and I get bored eating healthy foods. These are just a few of the many excuses or lies that have plagued my thoughts daily for years. Unfortunately, I believed these lies for so long I had lost hope.

Proverbs 13:12 NIV says, "Hope deferred makes the heart sick" and that's what having excuses did to me. Without even realizing it, I allowed these lies to be roadblocks to my weight loss success because they deferred, postponed, and put on hold any hope I ever had of accomplishing losing weight or any other goals.

This verse goes on to say, "… but a longing fulfilled is a tree of life." Through Teresa's amazing memoirs and excellent coaching, I am learning in order to have those longings fulfilled I must first acknowledge that Jesus is the vine. I am one of the branches, and apart from Him I can do nothing. I kept trying to do this weight loss journey on my own and using excuses was just a "good" way to justify my failed attempts.

This realization is helping me develop a *Sweet Hunger* for following Jesus. As I *Sweet Surrender* all my *Sweet Excuses* to Jesus, one-by-one, I am learning to rely on His *Sweet Grace*. I am also experiencing *Sweet Changes* that are causing me to form new habits that are continuously leading to weight loss on my *Sweet Journey to Transformation*. I could never do any of this on my own.

I am still a work in progress, but gleaning from Teresa's Spirit-led wisdom, I now have the hope more than ever that my *Sweet Freedom* is on its way.

One day soon I believe I will have victory and come to know very well that a longing fulfilled is a tree of life and sweet to the soul, just like she did!

I can't wait to read *Sweet Excuses*. I know it will be a great addition to Teresa's books and a big help to me and others.

LIFE-SAVING GROUP
Debbie Magner, Bradenton, FL

Teresa Shields Parker and her Overcomers Christian Weight Loss Academy have saved my life. When I met Teresa, it became apparent to me that my problem with overeating and my obsession with weight and food was a spiritual problem.

When the group started, it was so comforting to know I was not alone and others were and are struggling with the same issues. I am learning that in order to heal, I need to transform from the inside out. A closer walk with God is the solution to my problem.

Teresa and the group have been so insightful in my life, my habits, issues and most importantly, my relationships with the Father, Son, and Holy Spirit. I feel like a new woman from the one I was several years ago when I met Teresa.

This group is life-changing! I am so grateful to be a part of it! I am excited for everyone who will read her seventh book, *Sweet Excuses*.

HABIT CHANGE HELPED ME LOSE 80 POUNDS
Jay Lee, Sanford, FL

Teresa's first book, *Sweet Grace: How I Lost 250 Pounds and Stopped Trying to Earn God's Favor*, was the beginning of true change of habit for me.

That has resulted in a loss of over 80 pounds and counting. Teresa is honest about her own struggles spiritually on the way to her victory, especially with food.

Her approach is honest and down-to-earth. I am looking forward to reading her new book. If you have been fighting the battle of gaining control of food and losing weight, then this, *Sweet Excuses*, her seventh book, is for you.

DELIVERANCE FROM FOOD BONDAGE
Michele Gipp, Montrose CO

After a lifetime of living in slavery to food addiction and obesity, yoyo dieting, and letting emotions lead me to food for comfort, cope, and escape, I seriously cried out to God for deliverance from this bondage.

His answer came through Teresa Shields Parker's podcast, Sweet Grace for Your Journey. Listening for about three months,

I realized she had the real answers I had been looking for and I joined her Overcomer's Academy.

Teresa shares from her own experiences compassionately and honestly. As a coach, she's skilled in leading each participant through a transforming process that includes Biblical principles, habit changes, and practical steps to discovering and living in freedom.

I personally have lost 15 pounds and the scale continues to move down. More importantly, I have begun to gain so much more in navigating life without constantly being ruled by food!

My relationship with God has grown in fresh and exciting ways. Having my life changed from her excellent coaching, books, and group, I am looking forward to the gems in this new book, *Sweet Excuses*. I have no doubt it will be another enhancement in my arsenal against my food addiction issues.

WHY CAN'T I STOP EATING?
Cheri Garst Lowman, Prescott, AZ

"Why can't I stop eating?" I typed this into the Google search bar one night as tears filled my eyes and chips filled my mouth. The top search result was Teresa Shields Parker's podcast, Sweet Grace for Your Journey. I listened to the first episode and knew God had thrown me a lifeline.

Since joining Overcomers Academy, I have learned the roots of my overeating and steps to take to overcome the lifelong habits I have formed. I have learned techniques which have helped me connect to God in ways I never have before.

As a result, God has shown me some childhood hurts and healed them. I finally feel my value to God and that I am worth the effort it will take to have permanent lifestyle change. I am experiencing healing and change. I know that with the things I have learned, I will reach my goals.

CONVICTED
Linda Ordway, Columbia, MO

I have the honor of being one of several first readers for Teresa Shields Parker's books. I have spent the last 24 hours digesting her latest book, *Sweet Excuses*. I am convicted from my head down to my toes. God knows how to read my mail.

I am never really ready for what she writes because God always uses her to correct my course in a way I could never plan. She never knows what she is doing in the natural, but I get nailed right between the eyes. She is someone God uses to straighten my string.

My excuse was, "I am too stressed to stay healthy." God showed me I was slipping from the commitment I had made to Him and to myself. Several things happened that were out of my control.

It was easier to turn to sweets than to pray and trust in God. I was relying on the quick pick-me-up of sugar to make me feel better. Instead, I felt stiff, bloated, slow, and tired.

Now that I am convicted again, I am stepping back into the healthy lifestyle. Thanks, Teresa, for using your gift to help me get back on track. I appreciate what God did in you to help me be all that He has called me to be. Our gifts have been crossing each other for decades. I hope to be proofreading your books for decades to come. You are a life-changing blessing in my life.

GREAT TITLE FOR A GREAT BOOK!
Marilyn Goodson Logan, Columbia, MO

I have been privileged to be a first reader of all seven of Teresa Shields Parker's Sweet Series books. *Sweet Excuses* is great title for her newest book. It immediately drew me in to discover what it was all about, because making excuses for something I don't want to do comes so easily for me.

The more I read, the more I identified with what she was pointing out and the more I was discovering how to face my temptations and overcome them so that excuses would not be necessary.

Teresa effectively defines the excuses often used in a person's weight loss journey, exposes the lies behind them, and shows how applying specific Bible scriptures can help us overcome temptation and achieve success in reaching the goals we have set for ourselves.

I particularly loved the way she used various translations of scripture to illuminate the exact truth she was setting forth for the reader to grasp and implement in their own personal lives. This really made the scriptures I was already familiar with come alive in new ways.

This book will be a tool to go beyond making excuses and enable you to activate God's power to achieve the victory you are seeking. It is a great addition to her Sweet Series.

"We do not have the excuse of ignorance, everything—and I do mean everything—connected with that old way of life has to go."

EPHESIANS 4:22 MSg

CHAPTER 1

EXCUSES, EXCUSES

Excuses, excuses—we have them for everything especially losing weight and getting healthy. Why do we have excuses anyway? Why do we use them when we really do want to lose weight and get healthy? Why do we let them keep us from God's best? How can we put them in our past and move forward with what we know God wants for us?

An excuse is very similar to a stronghold because it has an element of truth to it. We all know deep down inside that an excuse is basically a lie designed to keep us from doing what we don't want to do but know we should do.

For 20 years, up until September of 2017, we were foster parents to developmentally delayed teens and young adults. Several we took care of were pathological liars. They believed their own lies. There was no way we could convince them that what they were saying was a lie even when we had all the evidence to back up the fact they were lying.

Many of us treat excuses the same way. We believe they are true and are the reasons we can't get out of debt, stop drinking, stop watching pornography, stop cheating on or lying to our spouse, stop drinking, stop overusing prescription drugs, stop using street drugs, or stop overeating. We have our excuses so well-honed that we believe they are 100 percent true. Because of them we will never be able to overcome whatever it is that is keeping us from moving forward.

EXCUSES ARE DANGEROUS

Excuses are dangerous because they keep us from doing what is best for us. An excuse helps us not put forth the effort to change. We want to continue to do what we are doing instead of what is best for us. An excuse feels a whole lot easier than going on a transformation journey.

This is dangerous for Christians because we are making excuses for why we can't follow God in some particular area. Following Him may feel too difficult or overwhelming, but that isn't a good enough excuse because we realize it makes us sound like wimps. So, we make up other more elaborate excuses we can live with. Many times, these excuses just help us continue to do what we've always done before.

In Ephesians 4:17–24 MSG Paul said, "I insist—and God backs me up on this—that there be no going along with the crowd, the empty-headed, mindless crowd. They've refused for so long to deal with God that they've lost touch not only with God but with reality itself. They can't think straight anymore. Feeling no pain, they let themselves go in sexual obsession, addicted to every sort of perversion (and anything else that is against what God says is best).

"But that's no life for you. You learned Christ! My assumption is that you have paid careful attention to Him, been well instructed in the truth precisely as we have it in Jesus. Since, then, we do not have the excuse of ignorance, everything—and I do mean everything—connected with that old way of life has to go. It's rotten through and through. Get rid of it!

"And then take on an entirely new way of life—a God-fashioned life, a life renewed from the inside and working itself into your conduct as God accurately reproduces His character in you."

When we are making excuses for what we know God wants us to do, we are not growing in Him. Spiritual growth should be an ongoing goal of every Christian. We develop excuses to convince ourselves that we can't do what God wants us to do, so it's OK to ignore how He's convicting us. We have this one area we turn a blind eye to. However, as Paul said in Ephesians 4:22 MSG, "We do not have the excuse of ignorance. Everything connected to our old way of life or the way of the world has to go."

RENEWED FROM THE INSIDE OUT

Our goal should be to live a God-fashioned life, renewed from the inside out. We must allow God to help us do away with our excuses because we want our conduct to reproduce God's character in us.

The first thing God requires of us is commitment to change whatever part of our lives are most disconcerting. For many women, that is their weight. On my journey, I've learned that

CHAPTER 1

my weight was just a wake-up call for me to focus on and re-examine my connection to God.

I thought my connection to Him was great. I quickly understood that if it was, I wouldn't have such an intense issue of holding foods made with sugar and flour in such high esteem. Without a solid connection to Him I wasn't able to hear what He was trying to tell me about my issue with food, which was that I was a sugar addict.

Any kind of food addiction is difficult to overcome because we need to eat. We just need to eat what is best for us and not use food as a companion, comfort, or protection. We may not even realize we are doing this. Or we may realize it but just think it's part of who we are.

For years, I felt my desire for certain foods was a part of me, like having brown eyes and freckles. I couldn't change it, and I didn't want to change it. I knew Psalms 139:13 TPT said, "You formed my innermost being, shaping my delicate inside and my intricate outside, and wove them all together in my mother's womb."

IT'S GOD'S FAULT!

My first huge excuse about why I ate all the things I wanted and couldn't help it was because God made me this way. It was the fallback excuse I would tell myself every time I went on a diet, lost weight, went off the diet when I reached my goal, began eating everything in sight, and gained the weight back plus more. My excuse was, "God, this is Your fault. You made me this way. So fix me. Make it so I can eat what I want and not gain weight."

It's ridiculous for us to blame God. That's like telling Him we know better than He does. "Who do you think you are to second-guess God? How could a human being molded out of clay say to the one who molded him, 'Why in the world did you make me this way?'" (Romans 9:20 TPT).

When I finally realized that my issue was sugar addiction, I began to understand that I am prone to addiction. I have been addicted to diet soda, sugary foods, breads, carbs, money, and work. Addiction may be part of my personality, but it does not have to be negative.

ADDICTED TO JESUS

My dad grew up with an alcoholic father and grandfather. All his uncles were also alcoholics. Many of his brothers were headed that way. Dad made a decision early in his life when he accepted Jesus at age nine that he would not fall into that mold. By the age of 16, he had chosen to be addicted to Jesus.

With that one decision, he opened the door of blessing in our family. He won every one of his brothers and his sister to Jesus. He became a pastor and so did one of his brothers. I look back over his life and realize the major impact his decision had and still has on my life. I am so proud of him that it makes me cry just thinking about it.

God knew my past. He knew my tendencies. He wanted me to take what had become a hinderance in my life and use it for good, like Dad did.

Remember that old Carman song, "Addicted to Jesus"? Here's a verse if you've forgotten:

CHAPTER 1

"People they go crazy and don't know when to stop

Running, jogging, exercising, I'm gonna pump you up

Smokin' in the boys room, drink up all the booze

Drug and crack and heart attack and what do you lose?

In common sight, crime at night, danger 'round the bend

No way out, yo, it's about being born again.

He paid your price, sacrifice, the cross of Calvary

It's done, be one, and you can be free

Stand tall, stand tall, stand strong, stand strong

Say it loud, say it loud, say it along

Bust the Devil up in pieces

Get alive with God

Addicted to Jesus."

That should be my theme song. I need to add a line that says, "eating everything I see because it's what I be." I don't want to be addicted to sugar or food. I want to be addicted to Jesus. It should be every Christian's goal.

I do not have the right to question God. God did not make me the way I became. I did that myself by not listening to Him in the first place. That is even more scary than blaming Him.

James said, "When you are tempted don't ever say, 'God is tempting me,' for God is incapable of being tempted by evil and He is never the source of temptation. Instead, it is each person's own desires and thoughts that drag them into evil and lure them away into darkness. Evil desires give birth to evil actions. And when sin is fully mature it can murder you!" (James 1:13-15 TPT).

The same verses in the Message version put it this way, "Don't let anyone under pressure to give in to evil say, 'God is trying to trip me up.' God is impervious to evil, and puts evil in no one's way. The temptation to give in to evil comes from us and only us. We have no one to blame but the leering, seducing flare-up of our own lust. Lust gets pregnant, and has a baby: sin! Sin grows up to adulthood, and becomes a real killer."

The New International Version of James 1:15 says, "Then, after desire has conceived, it gives birth to sin; and sin, when it is full-grown, gives birth to death."

Giving in to any temptation is our fault. We have allowed our desires to grow inside of us. As the Message said, "The temptation ... comes from us and only us." It has become something we want, something we feel we need in order to live, or something we think we have a right to continue to indulge in. We don't want to go through what we know it will take to say, "no" to the sugary treats which have become so tempting that they are a part of our lives.

> Sin grows up to adulthood and becomes a real killer.

Back in 1977, I read Matthew 17:20 where Jesus answered the disciples by saying, "'You don't have enough faith,' Jesus told them. 'I tell you the truth, if you had faith even as small as a mustard seed, you could say to this mountain, 'Move from here to there,' and it would move. Nothing would be impossible.'"

I told God, "I have a mountain of weight on my body and a little bit of faith. How can this mountain be moved?" I was 24 years old and had just topped 200 pounds for the first time

CHAPTER 1

in my life. God answered, "Stop eating sugar. Eat more meat, fruits, and vegetables. And stop eating so much bread."

If I had done that back then, I would have never gained up to 430 pounds. Instead of doing what He told me to do, like the stubborn person I was, I said, "Great plan, God. If I did that I would lose weight, but I can't do that. I can't stop eating sugar."

I CAN'T STOP EATING SUGAR

That's another excuse. "I can't stop eating sugar." I didn't ask Him to show me how to do that. I just said, "I can't." That also involved yet another excuse. "I shouldn't have to stop eating all sugar. Everyone else can eat it. I should be able to as well."

Perhaps I could have been able to if I could have mitigated the amount of sugar I ate, but with sugar it's all or nothing for me. Sugar is very much like alcohol to some people. What do alcoholics use to get off alcohol? Many use sugary treats. They are replacing one addiction for another.

My big issue was I didn't want to have to do the work I knew it would take to stop indulging in sugar. It was all my fault, but I was making excuses as to why I couldn't follow what God wanted me to do. I was selfish and wanted what I wanted. As a self-indulged individual, I thought God was supposed to give me what I wanted.

Jesus had a different view on that. In Luke 9:23-25 TPT, "He said to all of His followers, 'If you truly desire to be My disciple, you must disown your life completely, embrace My 'cross' as your own, and surrender to My ways. For if you choose self-sacrifice, giving up your lives for My glory, you will discover true life.

EXCUSES, EXCUSES

"But if you choose to keep your lives for yourselves, you will lose what you try to keep. Even if you gained all the wealth and power of this world, and all the things it could offer you, yet lost your soul in the process, what good is that?'"

Luke 9:23 AMP translates the words that say, "we must disown ourselves" as we must "set aside our selfish interests." I know my main selfish interest for most of my life was eating whatever I wanted, whenever I wanted, and excusing it as what I have to do in order to survive.

John 14:15 MSG tells us we must obey God in order to show our love for Him. Jesus said, "If you love Me, show it by doing what I've told you." Then He added in John 14:23 MSG, "If anyone loves Me, He will carefully keep My word and My Father will love him—we'll move right into the neighborhood! Not loving Me means not keeping My words."

> Roll up your sleeves, get your head in the game, be totally ready to receive the gift that's coming.

This theme continued in 1 Peter 1:14-15 MSG. "So roll up your sleeves, get your head in the game, be totally ready to receive the gift that's coming when Jesus arrives.

"Don't lazily slip back into those old grooves of evil, doing just what you feel like doing. You didn't know any better then. You do now. As obedient children, let yourselves be pulled into a way of life shaped by God's life, a life energetic and blazing with holiness."

It is so easy to slip back into old habits that do not benefit us. The other day, I went to the pool to exercise for the first time since a surgery had sidelined me. Since it was lunch time, I decided to get a grilled chicken and a diet soda. I hadn't had a diet soda in years. They are very addictive to me and always make me want sugar because they mimic sugar.

Providentially, I had to stop at a stoplight. It was then I realized I hadn't asked God about this. I said out loud, "God, is it OK for me to have a diet soda or should I have water?"

Immediately, 1 Corinthians 6:12 NIV came to mind. "'I have the right to do anything,' you say—but not everything is beneficial. 'I have the right to do anything'—but I will not be mastered by anything."

Even a so-called "diet" soft drink will master me if I let it. It is basically comprised of chemicals, so it is not beneficial for me like cold water. I said, "OK God. Cold refreshing water it is and will be from now on."

What does God want for us? Only what is beneficial. How much of what you eat is beneficial? It's always good to remind yourself of this when temptation comes. Trust me, when you are trying to do the right thing, temptation will come.

PRAY THIS PRAYER

"Jesus, I want to be addicted to only You. I am well aware of other addictions that want to master me—sugar, work, money, and anything else that looks appealing.

"Today I turn my back on all those things. Jesus, I choose You. I choose to believe You know what's best for me. I will no longer blame my failures on You.

"I choose to listen to what You want for me. I choose to listen to You and You alone. In Your name, Amen.

EXCUSES, EXCUSES

ANSWER THESE QUESTIONS

1. In your opinion, what is an excuse?

2. Why are excuses dangerous for Christians?

3. What is one thing God has told you to do that you haven't done yet?

4. What is your excuse for not doing that?

5. What are some other excuses you have? List all you can think of.

6. What would it look like for you to be addicted to Jesus?

7. How much of what you eat is beneficial for you?

CHAPTER 1

ENDNOTES

1. Liciardello, Carman. Lyrics to "Addicted to Jesus." https://genius.com/Carman-addicted-to-jesus-lyrics/

CHAPTER 2

PROCRASTINATION IS AN EXCUSE

When we are procrastinating, we are just making excuses for why we aren't doing what we know we should be doing. To procrastinate is to delay or put off doing something. An excuse is coming up with a reason to put off doing something. Basically, it's the same thing.

I have heard many different reasons (or excuses) for why someone would procrastinate about losing weight. One big one is I need to take care of my family or others. It's the caregiver excuse. We put off taking care of ourselves because we haven't been successful at that. We take care of others or do things for others because there is an instant gratification in doing that.

If that's you, you may have said things like I don't have time to work on myself. I would rather spend time with others than work on myself. I'm not important enough to work on me. I'll just fail, so let me do something I can do.

However, in Mark 12:30-31 NLT Jesus said, "You must love the Lord your God with all your heart, all your soul, all your mind, and all your strength.' The second is equally important:

CHAPTER 2

'Love your neighbor as yourself.' No other commandment is greater than these."

Those with the helper mentality might use these verses to justify how important it is to prioritize doing things for others, but wait a minute. It says to love others as you love yourself.

If we aren't taking care of ourselves, we aren't loving ourselves. That means if we are trying to love others like we love ourselves, we aren't doing a very good job of either.

> If we are trying to love others like we love ourselves but aren't taking care of ourselves, we aren't doing a good job of either.

It's really an excuse for not doing what we know God wants us to do. When I was super morbidly obese, I had my time filled to the brim doing volunteer work, serving on boards, teaching classes, and joining groups. I had something to do all the time.

Why was I doing that instead of working on my obvious problem? I had been on every diet trying to lose weight on my own and it didn't work. I'd lose weight and when I got to goal weight, I'd celebrate by eating something sugary and decadent. That would cause me to gain the weight back again, plus more. Diets were only making me gain weight instead of lose weight.

So. I helped where I could doing what I could. I knew I was trying to force myself to do things for God that were good works. Even though they were good things none were my passion. I knew that, but I felt I had stepped out of my passion of writing when the Christian newspaper I was publishing folded.

Maybe I was trying to find something to fill that void, but nothing was working because I was in big-time procrastination mode from doing what I knew down deep inside God wanted me to do. That was to find out how to lose weight and keep it off. Any time that subject came to mind I put it aside and said, like the famous procrastinator Scarlett O'Hara, "I'll not think about that today. I'll think about that tomorrow."[1] And of course tomorrow never seemed to come.

> Can this battle ever be won? Yes, but not in your own strength.

One might think running around keeping busy was good for me and would keep me from overeating, but just the opposite was true. I was stressed to the max doing things I thought were good things but were not the main thing God wanted for me.

I was doing all these things to look good to God when all God wanted was for me to begin to take care of myself. I needed desperately to do that because in addition to the weight on my 5' 5" frame, I had congestive heart failure, diabetes, high blood pressure, and could barely walk.

One woman shared with me that she felt like her food addiction was keeping her in a daily prison. She said that the battle she was in was consuming her and destroying her life. She asked a simple question, "Can this battle ever be won?"

My answer to her and to those who feel the same way is yes, but not in your own strength. It can only be won by

CHAPTER 2

surrendering completely to Jesus and letting Him lead you on your journey.

Transformation is possible but only when we rely on Jesus to help us. "I can do everything through Christ who gives me strength" (Phil 4:13 NLT). Many times, we under-emphasize the last part of that verse. The first part is null and void though, without the fact that it is Christ Jesus who is the powerhouse in all we attempt to do.

PLENTY OR LITTLE

Another version stated it this way, "I find that the strength of Christ's explosive power infuses me to conquer every difficulty" (Philippians 4:13 TPT). Before that Philippians 4:12 TPT said, "I know how to live on almost nothing or with everything. I have learned the secret of living in every situation, whether it is with a full stomach or empty, with plenty or little."

Paul wrote these words from prison. Likely, he was very hungry. It's the only reason I know of for him to write about food. However, he is speaking right to where we live. Because the next verse is Philippians 4:13 which gives us the secret that we need to stop the excuses. That secret is the strength and power of Jesus.

I had been telling myself I couldn't lose weight. This was partly true. I couldn't lose weight as long as I was eating foods made with sugar and flour. My husband can stop with one cookie. I can't. It just is not possible for me.

So, when God revealed to me that I was a sugar addict, I connected the dots. An alcoholic is addicted to alcohol. To stop that addiction, she must stop drinking alcohol. If I am a sugar addict then I must stop eating sugar. The problem was I didn't know how to do that.

With every diet I had been on, I had stopped sugar for a season and had lost weight, but I always had the goal of eating it again. It would be my reward at the end of a difficult, self-imposed restriction. I had done this probably six times in my life. The truth was, I could lose weight if I didn't eat anything made with sugar. As much as I wanted to follow God and do the right thing, I didn't know how to stop eating sugar for the rest of my life.

What I learned through my transformation journey is this is a process. My first step in the process was true heartfelt repentance and surrender to God. I had told God I was sorry and had repented many times, but this was totally different.

This was a deep, gut-wrenching anguish cry of surrender. I mourned what I had done to my body. I surrendered everything to Jesus. I told Him I was done with trying to do things my way. I asked Him to show me how to surrender sugar, not just for a while, but for the rest of my life. I admitted I was a sugar addict and wanted that substance gone from my life.

> This was a deep, gut-wrenching anguish cry of surrender. I mourned what I had done to my body.

I had no idea how He could help me, but deep inside I knew this was a turning point. I knew from that day on I would never be the same.

The first thing that happened was I started going to a group my mentor led. It is my firm conviction that every food or sugar addict needs to be a part of a group that will help them understand why food and sugar addiction is totally different from a diet.

My mentor, who had been through addiction, helped me understand I had deeply ingrained habits that were keeping me returning to food for things like comfort, companionship, and protection.

In order to break these habits, I had to begin with some small, simple bad habit and stop doing that while starting a new good habit. I had to focus on the new habit and put firm boundaries around the bad habit. This was difficult in the beginning, but once I got the hang of it, it worked miracles in my life.

> Small successes are great motivators.

I also learned that small successes are great motivators. The small stop-start I began was something that was very doable for me. I stopped eating candy, which I was able to do easily even though it had been a trigger food, and started to exercise three times a week. These are habits I still have.

Part of the reason this worked for me was because I left sugar in God's hands in that initial surrender time. Then I followed my mentor's advice about how to get sugar out of my life for good. We also had weekly accountability meetings, which were extremely important for me.

Another thing I did was to resign from every board and every volunteer job I was involved in. Instead, I chose to focus on myself. I got a trainer. I went to exercise five times a week. I saw doctors and nutritionists. I went to my weekly group meetings. I did daily Bible study and time with God. I still had mentally challenged foster clients we were taking care of, but I had staff to whom I turned over most everything. For the very first time in my life, the focus was on me.

I am from the era where we learned the acronym JOY which meant Jesus first, Others second, and Yourself last. I began to realize that is not Biblical at all. It has to be JMO. Even though that spells nothing, it changed everything for me. Jesus first, Myself second, and then I am able to help Others.

> JMO not JOY. Jesus first, Myself second, and then I am able to help others.

Working on ourselves should be our first priority. Sadly, I know those who put others before themselves and cut their lives short because they were the ones who cooked the meals and wanted to please everyone with the kinds of foods they had always cooked. Those meals might have been OK for their family, but they weren't for themselves.

We can't put off the important stuff. Solomon said in Proverbs 6:4 NLT, "Don't put it off; do it now! Don't rest until you do."

Then, Proverbs 24:12 NLT adds not to excuse ourselves by saying, "'Look, we didn't know.' For God understands all hearts, and He sees you. He who guards your soul knows you knew. He will repay all people as their actions deserve."

Every person I talk to about overeating knows they have a problem with food. They know they need to be doing something about it, but they make excuses to procrastinate doing anything. This does nothing to help the problem and everything to prolong it.

The habit change process really helps with this. We start small and slow and learn how committed we really are. Can we do this one small thing to help ourselves for the rest of our lives? It's usually the all or nothing diet plans that trip us up. We can do them, but only for a certain length of time.

EXCUSES ARE THE WAY WE PROCRASTINATE

Excuses have become the way we procrastinate. Well-known Bible teacher and speaker, Joyce Meyer says, "Don't give into excuses that can keep you from really living the best life God has for you!" Why is it that we resist the things we know will help us in order to get what we want? We want to be healthy and live the best life for God. So why are we putting off doing something about it?

One of our founding fathers, Benjamin Franklin, said, "He that is good for making excuses is seldom good for anything else." Author Alan Maiccon added, "Be stronger than your strongest excuse. Be greater than your most negative voice!" Do you realize that you are not living your best life now because you are allowing some half-lie excuse to rule your life?

Motivational Speaker and Author Steve Mariboli laid it on the line when he said, "Your complaints, your drama, your victim mentality, your whining, your blaming, and all of your excuses have never gotten you even a single step closer to your goals or dreams. Let go of your nonsense. Let go of the delusion that you deserve better and go earn it! Today is a new day! We may place blame, give reasons, and even have excuses; but in the end, it is an act of cowardice to not follow your dreams."

Florence Nightingale, founder of the modern nursing movement, attributed her success to one thing. "I never gave or took an excuse." Dave Del Dotto, a real estate investor, added, "No one ever excused his way to success."

Finally, Roy Bennett, Zimbabwean politician, speaking about change said, "Maturity is when you stop complaining and making excuses in your life. You realize everything that happens in life is a result of the previous choice you've made and start making new choices to change your life."

For those of us whose main failure is overeating, that failure is the same as sin, especially if we've had a clear word from God about it.

Psalms 39:6-9 TPT says, "We live our lives like those living in shadows. All our activities and energies are spent for things that pass away.

"We gather, we hoard, we cling to our things, only to leave them all behind for who knows who. And now, God, I'm left with one conclusion: my only hope is to hope in You alone!

> Lord, I'm left speechless and I have no excuse, so I'll not complain any longer.

"Save me from being overpowered by my sin; don't make me a disgrace before the degenerate. Lord, I'm left speechless and I have no excuse, so I'll not complain any longer."

One big way we can help ourselves is to join a group with others who have issues like we have and a coach who has overcome those issues.

It is not the right group unless the focus is squarely on God helping us through this issue. For procrastinators the big problem is usually not joining a group but taking advantage of all a group has to offer.

CHAPTER 2

In my Overcomers Christian Weight Loss Academy, we have a weekly Encouragement Room time, monthly Zoom calls, 25 courses in our learn dashboard, and a Facebook group where members can ask any question any time.

Any group will not help anyone, though, if they don't take advantage of the resources. I want those with food issues to join the group, but I want them to be really committed when they do.

We have the God of the universe on our side. So. what is the problem? Us and our excuses are all that stands in our way. It's time to get to work and do what God is calling us to do. Procrastination has to go. Make the next right step.

PRAY THIS PRAYER

"Dear Jesus, I pray for myself as I am battling the issue of overeating, binging and food addiction. I feel stuck in a prison of food I cannot manage.

"I have given up. Excuses reign supreme and keep me stuck in a cycle of procrastination, like a hamster on a treadmill.

"Breakthrough for me today, Lord. Set me free.

"In Your precious name I pray, Amen."

ANSWER THESE QUESTIONS

1. What does procrastination mean to you?

2. What things do you procrastinate about? List them all.

3. Do you procrastinate when God tells you to do something, or do you question Him endlessly and perhaps never get around to it? When was the last time you did this?

4. How does procrastination keep you in a daily prison?

5. What verse is most helpful to you in order to start moving from procrastination to transformation?

6. What needs to be your next right step?

7. When will you do that? Set a date and a time to get that done.

CHAPTER 2

ENDNOTE

1. Selznick International Pictures, Metro-Goldwyn-Mayer. (1939). Gone With the Wind.

CHAPTER 3

I WANT WHAT I WANT

There's no one in the world more adamant than two-year-olds who want their favorite candies. They know what they want, and they want it now! "Wait until after lunch" or "No," do not seem to be in the realm of things they understand.

Of course, as good parents, we know we have to set limits when they are young and not give in or they will be eating candy any time the desire hits. This sets up a precedent for allowing our selfish desires and cravings to lead us for the rest of our lives. It definitely did in my life. Both the withholding of candy and the unlimited access to sweets had a huge impact on me.

When we are following our desires and cravings we aren't living with and by the power of the Holy Spirit. In Galatians 5:16-18 TPT Paul told us how important surrendering to God is. "As you yield to the dynamic life and power of the Holy Spirit, you will abandon the cravings of your self-life. When your self-life craves the things that offend the Holy Spirit you hinder Him from living free within you!

"And the Holy Spirit's intense cravings hinder your self-life from dominating you! So then, the two incompatible and conflicting forces within you are your self-life of the flesh and the new creation life of the Spirit. But when you yield to the life of the Spirit, you will no longer be living under the law, but soaring above it!"

When we do what we want, we are not following the Holy Spirit. We are allowing our cravings to lead us. The solution is to surrender to the Holy Spirit. Then Jesus told us in Luke 9:23 AMP, "If anyone wishes to follow Me, he must deny himself, set aside selfish interests, and take up his cross daily and follow Me."

CARAMEL HEAVEN

Wanting what I wanted started early for me. When I was about five, I became aware that my mother had a bag of caramels up in the kitchen cabinet. I loved caramels, but they were off-limits to me. So when she would take a nap in her bedroom, I'd pull a chair up to the counter, climb up and snitch a caramel.

At first, I was very careful. I only took one at time. However, I soon wanted more and what I wanted, I felt I had to have. I thought my mind was telling me I needed candy. If my body desired it then I must need it. This went on for about a year until I was in school all day and wasn't home during my mother's afternoon nap.

One time in the summer, though, I had to have a caramel. Mom was asleep. I crept up on the counter, but this time I took the entire bag down because there weren't many caramels in there. I sat in the middle of the floor indulging myself, not being aware of anything else in the room. I was in caramel heaven until I looked over and saw my mother's shoes in front of me. Her left foot was tapping. I didn't even have to look up. I knew her arms were crossed, and she was frowning down at me over her glasses.

"Teresa Kay," she said. "What do you think you are doing?"

I looked up, "I was hungry."

"Are those your caramels?" she asked.

I shook my head, "No."

"The caramels are mine and you are never to eat them again without permission. When you get to be an adult, you can buy your own candy and eat as much as you want. But right now, you aren't to touch these."

She grabbed the bag with the few remaining pieces and took it to her room where she carefully stashed it so I couldn't find it.

CHEWING ON TAFFY

Another time Dad brought home a bag of saltwater taffy. He left it on the kitchen counter. I wanted some so I grabbed the bag and took it to the bathroom with me, which was the only place I could be alone.

I was only going to eat a few pieces, but I wound up staying in the bathroom way too long chewing on taffy. Dad knocked on the door and asked what I was doing.

I said, "Nothing."

"Come out then. I need to get in there."

"I can't get the door open," I lied as I tried to scoop the candy back in the bag and throw away the wrappers at the same time. He opened the door, took one look at the candy, and took the bag from me.

Dad didn't chastise me for what I'd done. He was willing to share his candy with us, but he was more careful about putting it away from then on.

WORKING FOR COOKIES

It seemed from as far back as I can remember, sweets were what I wanted. That desire didn't go away as I got older and stayed more often with my grandparents on their farm. There, Grandma always had me help her make a big batch of oatmeal cookies. We'd eat them until they were all gone and then make another batch the next day.

She worked hard and I worked with her, gathering eggs, getting vegetables from the garden, breaking green beans, and hulling peas. I helped her cook breakfast, lunch, and supper, as well as doing the laundry in the old wringer washing machine down in the basement. We worked, but I didn't mind it because we ate well.

My reward when I went to Grandma's was all the sweets I wanted. I also loved all of her cooking, especially hoecake and fresh breads. Country fried steak, gravy, and mashed potatoes was one of my favorite meals that she made.

It just made sense to me that when I grew up and began living first as a single and then as a married woman, I cooked all the things Grandma had taught me to cook. The one thing I made most often, though, was her oatmeal cookies. I could make a batch and eat all those cookies in a few hours. Then I'd have to bake more because the house smelled like oatmeal cookies, but there were none to be found.

I felt if I wanted something sweet to eat, I was following my mother's advice. I was now an adult, and I could eat all the candy I wanted and eat I did. However, I also kept gaining weight. I wanted to lose weight, but I also wanted to keep eating the foods I loved.

The foods I loved had a hold on me. So, when I asked God how to lose weight and He told me I was going to have to stop eating sugar and flour, and eat more meats, fruits, and vegetables, I dismissed His advice. I was still going by what I thought as a kid. If my body craved certain foods, then I was going to eat them.

WEIGHED ON A FREIGHT SCALE

I continued to eat that way, while dieting off and on, losing weight and gaining it all back plus more until about 1999 when I discovered I weighed 430 pounds. The only reason I know what I weighed then was because I was in the hospital. They took me down to the loading dock and weighed me on a freight scale. It was embarrassing. I had lost some weight, so I know I weighed even more at some point.

This was the time the cardiac surgeon came in my hospital room and told me I didn't need to have open heart surgery like he originally thought. He said, "You have congestive heart failure. Your body is too big for your heart. You need to lose at least 100 pounds and keep it off or you will be dead in five years." Then, he turned and walked out of the room.

This should have catapulted me into motion. I should have been eager to do whatever I could to lose the weight. The problem was I didn't want to live without eating whatever I wanted, but I also didn't want to die. I wanted God to fix me so I could eat what I wanted and still lose weight. I was smart. I knew that wouldn't happen, but a girl can hope for a magic cure, can't she?

As I lay there in that hospital bed I thought of my beautiful daughter, amazing son, and loving husband. Jenny, my daughter, was nine. Andrew, my son, was 15. I knew if I died my husband would take care of them. However, they would be without a mother's care and love. By that time both my mother and grandmother had passed away. My daughter needed me.

I wanted to be there for all of them, but I especially knew Jenny needed me to be there for her. She needed a mother in her life. I needed to get healthy for her. I also knew there were things God still had for me to do on this earth.

LIFE OR DEATH?

This time in my life was pivotal because it was the first time I had been told unabashedly that my extreme weight could lead to an early death. Other doctors had mentioned diets, but none had come out and laid the truth on the line as fearlessly as the rude cardiac surgeon had.

He opened my eyes to the dangers my over-indulgence in delicious foods and to my excuse that I wanted them simply because I loved to eat them had on my life. The other doctors were nicer about the fact I needed to lose weight, but they didn't deal in as many life and death matters as the cardiac surgeon. And not one of them had ever been overweight, much less super morbidly obese.

One sent me to a dietitian who sat me at a table with plastic food and what to me was a tiny plate, much smaller than I ever used. She showed me how much meat, vegetables, and fruits I should eat in relation to the plate size. There was no room left so where did the breads, potatoes, and desserts go? Oh, they must be on another plate because I felt I would never survive on that small amount of food. It was just another excuse because I wanted to eat what I wanted.

I did want to live. I just didn't want to give up the foods I loved. I really thought I couldn't survive without them. Romans 7:19 NLT described my mindset. "I want to do what is good, but I don't. I don't want to do what is wrong, but I do it anyway."

After my encounter with the rude cardiac surgeon, though, I did decide to go on a diet I'd been on before and lost 100 pounds. This time I said I would not reward myself with sugary treats after I lost the weight.

> I did want to live. I just didn't want to give up the foods I loved. I felt I couldn't live without them.

I'm a really good dieter. When I set my mind to it, I can lose weight, but I'd always gain it back plus more when I reached my goal. I decided this time, I would use my willpower and attempt to not do that again. I lost 100 pounds, and the cardiac surgeon was happy with me. I took that as a signal to start sampling my favorite desserts. Before long, I was back where I had been.

My story is long and involved, but I want you to understand that one of the main excuses I used to not do what God told me to do was that I craved foods made with sugar. I loved them. I lived for candy, cookies, brownies, sweet breads, and desserts of all kinds. Everything I ate seemed to have sugar and flour

CHAPTER 3

in it to some degree, even casseroles and main dishes tasted better with those two ingredients.

I could make a meal strictly off desserts and be extremely happy. How does one gain up to 430 pounds and beyond? Eat that way and you will definitely get there.

EXCUSES AND REASONS

An excuse is different from a reason. An excuse is mostly a lie. A reason is a truth. We all have reasons we don't do certain things. I don't eat sugar today because I know I am an addict. If f I start eating anything with high sugar content, it will be very difficult for me to stop.

That's not an excuse for not eating it. It is a reason because it is a truth. However, me saying I have to eat sugar because I want it? That's an excuse. I didn't have to eat it, so it was an excuse plain and simple.

I've weighed 430 pounds and I never want to go back there. Even when I was recovering from knee surgery and learning to walk all over again, I felt 10 times better than I did at that weight. Walking is an entirely different story when you are carrying at least 250 extra pounds. I really don't know how I did it.

I was being interviewed for a Christian television show. The interviewer was a woman. She asked, "When you were so large who enabled you to gain so much weight?" She meant who brought me my food.

I told her. "No one enabled me. I could walk, drive, work, go to the grocery store, cook food. I enabled myself. I knew exactly what I was doing."

This is so sad, but it is truer that true. I was good at making excuses for why I was eating myself to death, but I was the only one to blame.

Even though I hate the word and it is one of the seven deadly sins, I realized I was greedy. I always thought that a greedy person was someone who hoarded money. According to the dictionary greed is "a selfish or excessive desire for more than is needed or deserved especially of money, wealth, or food."

I definitely qualified as greedy. I wanted more food than I needed or deserved. At church dinners or family reunions I would go through the dessert line first to be sure to get what I wanted. Another sad but true confession.

Romans 7:19 NLT explained why we do these kinds of things. "I want to do what is good, but I don't. I don't want to do what is wrong, but I do it anyway."

Paul then asked a pivotal question and gave us the answer. "Oh, what a miserable person I am! Who will free me from this life that is dominated by sin and death? Thank God! The answer is in Jesus Christ our Lord. So you see how it is. In my mind I really want to obey God's law, but because of my sinful nature I am a slave to sin" (Romans 7:24 NLT).

JESUS IS THE ANSWER

Jesus is the answer. When we accept Him, we receive the Holy Spirit. He is within us to lead and guide us, but we have to acknowledge His presence and ask for His help. Jesus said in John 14:16-17 NIV, "And I will ask the Father, and He will give you another advocate (helper, comforter) to help you and be with you forever—the Spirit of truth.

CHAPTER 3

"The world cannot accept Him, because it neither sees Him nor knows Him. But you know Him, for He lives with you and will be in you."

We have the Holy Spirit so we also have the power of God to produce as a by-product of godliness, the fruit of the Spirit. Galatians 5:22-23 NLT says, "But the Holy Spirit produces this kind of fruit in our lives: love, joy, peace, patience, kindness, goodness, faithfulness, gentleness, and self-control. There is no law against these things!"

> Self-control is not about willpower or self-effort on our part. It is about total and complete surrender to the Holy Spirit.

One of the parts of the fruit of the Spirit is the one we always think we don't have—self-control. Still, if we are Christians, we already have self-control because we have the Holy Spirit and, therefore, we have the fruit of the Spirit. We only have to call on the Holy Spirit for His power to be activated in our lives.

Self-control is not a result of willpower on our part, but a result of surrendering to the Holy Spirit in our lives. We show self-control by crucifying our flesh in the areas we see as becoming addictive. Then, we ask the Holy Spirit for His guidance on how to master our desires and appetites and we do what He says.

Self-control is not about self-effort. That is the perversion of this fruit of the Spirit. It is about being Spirit-controlled, sensitive to His direction, guidance, and leading. It rests in God's work in our lives. We cooperate with or work with God in the accomplishing of His aims. In other words, we have to take the fork out of our mouths. We have to put the food down. He won't do it for us.

We cannot be passive in the exercise of self-control, but the Holy Spirit has to be the director. He is the One who initiates and guides us. Any discipline is not a result of self-effort but of us allowing the Holy Spiritto control us. As we surrender to Him completely, the Holy Spirit becomes our strengthener and energizer.

When I surrendered to the Holy Spirit, everything changed in my life. I promise, it will in yours, as well.

PRAY THIS PRAYER

"Holy Spirit, I have been selfish in my desire for what I want. I filled my stomach with things I craved, desired, and wanted more than I wanted You.

"I was not listening to You or allowing You to guide me. I had not surrendered to allow myself to be Spirit-controlled.

"I am so sorry, God. Please lead and guide me in how to change my desires into what You desire for me. Lead me Holy Spirit and I will follow.

"In Jesus' name I pray. Amen."

ANSWER THESE QUESTIONS

1. What do you want that you are not willing to give up?

CHAPTER 3

2. Is this something that is beneficial to you?

3. Galatians 5:22-23 lists the fruit of the Spirit. How can you experience more of these attributes in your life?

4. Galatians 5:16-18 talk about yielding to the dynamic life and power of the Holy Spirit. Is this something you want? If so, write a prayer telling God what you desire or thanking Him for leading you to yield completely to Him.

5. What was your relationship with sweets or other foods when you were growing up? Write a paragraph about that.

6. If God told you that He wanted you to stop eating sugar, desserts, chips, or the food that you love the most, could you do it? What might that be?

7. What are the dangers facing you if you don't lose weight and keep it off? Journal your thoughts.

CHAPTER 4

I'M AFRAID OF FAILURE

"It's going to be too hard. I might fail so I don't even want to start trying."

"I have to be strong for too long. My strength will give out. I've tried many times in the past and failed."

"I've always been fat. I'll always be fat. Nothing works. So why try?"

Those comments are from real-live brave souls who shared their excuses for not even trying to lose weight. Can you relate?

Failure is the topic that seems to be on every person's mind who has ever tried to lose weight. I blame the diet mentality and false advertising for a lot of this. Diets promise quick weight loss because that's what we want. We want to fix the outside and do it now, but God is all about fixing us first on the inside in our hearts, minds, souls, and spirits. This is where the desire to eat resides.

Until we get to the root of why we overeat, we will always gain the weight back and add more on. In other words, we will be stuck in the gain-lose-gain cycle. Yes, people lose weight on diets. Some, like me, lose lots of weight on diets. That's because we eat next to nothing in order to lose weight. For me, it was always 100 pounds. Then we reach the goal and gain it all back plus more when we start eating what we want or think we have to have.

Nothing makes you feel like a failure like losing 100 pounds, buying an entirely new wardrobe in the smaller size, and gaining all that weight back plus more. Then you have to buy more clothes in a larger size. I have done that at least six times during my life.

> I just won't try because failing is too much for me to take. I will just be fat and happy.

Finally, I just threw up my hands and said, "I give up! I can't lose weight. I am just a failure. If I don't try, I won't fail. So I just won't try because failing is too much for me to take. I will just be fat and happy." That didn't work either because I found out I wasn't happy being fat. So I ate to relieve the unhappiness. That made me gain more weight which made me feel like more of a failure.

When I finally did lose weight, I didn't do it to look better. I did it to honor God with my body and become healthier so I can serve Him better. Those should be our main reasons for embarking on this journey.

Another reason God wanted me to do this was to help others become healthier so they can also serve Him longer, too. He showed me the evil one is using the desire for more and more food as a weapon against God's people. We understand that we shouldn't indulge in alcohol, drugs, pornography, gambling, overspending, or other vices. However, everyone has to eat, don't they? So we overindulge in food and call it the sanctified sin.

When I weighed 430 pounds, I saw myself as a miserable failure as a woman, wife, mother, and friend. I couldn't walk very far. I was constantly exhausted. I was stressed, overwhelmed, and angry most of the time.

Just try walking with 250 extra pounds on your body. Think about it. That's five 50-pound bags of sand. I don't think I could even move a 25-pound bag. Yet, for years I lived carrying that amount of extra weight on my body.

AM I A FAILURE?

Am I failure? Oh, I can go down the road with the best of them. I can beat myself up all day for what I did to myself. Then I realized God uses our failures, as well as our successes to help us. A very familiar verse tells us this. We just have to read between the lines to understand it. "We know that in all things God works for the good of those who love Him, who have been called according to His purpose" (Romans 8:28 NIV).

Notice that it says God works in all things. It's not only in all the successes and accolades that He works to bring good from our lives. He works through our failures, trials, temptations, and defeats, too. God, who stands outside of time, has already seen all of our failures and factored them into how He's going to create something good out of our lives.

Had I listened to God in 1977 when He told me to stop eating sugar and bread, I wouldn't have gained up to 430 pounds. I wouldn't have had to surrender completely to the mercy of

God to help me lose 250 pounds and keep it off. If I hadn't lost the weight, I wouldn't be coaching others and they wouldn't be allowing God to help them overcome their food issues. I wouldn't be doing the job God called me to and which I love.

I am not happy that I gained the weight and not happy that I had to go through the process of losing it. I am happy I learned how to change my habits, give up sugar and gluten, and get closer to God than I ever have been. I could say I'm a failure for becoming super morbidly obese. If I had stopped trying at that point I definitely would be a failure today. Instead, I worked through that failure label and allowed God to show me what to do.

FAILURE IS A GREAT TEACHER

It's from my failures I have learned the most. Failure is our best teacher. We remember our lessons best when we have failed. I love words today because I spectacularly failed my spelling test in second grade when I put all the answers in the wrong place. Of course, like any seven-year-old I cried big tears about it in front of the whole class. What a failure, but today you bet I know how to spell and how to put the right words in the right places.

Dr. Ben Carson, former director of Pediatric Neurosurgery at the Johns Hopkins Children's Center and former U.S. Department of Urban Development secretary, said it best. "Success is determined not by whether or not you face obstacles but by your reaction to them. If you look at these obstacles as a containing fence, they become your excuse for failure. If you look at them as a hurdle, each one strengthens you for the next."

We love using our continued failure on diet after diet as an excuse not to try again. If we look at our failures as an opportunity to learn how to do better, then when we face the same issue again we can't help but succeed.

My issue was doing the same thing over and over again. Part of that was because I was following the diet mentality. I was doing everything in my own self-effort. I wasn't asking for or relying on God for His strength to help me.

> I was doing everything in my own self-effort. I wasn't asking for or relying on God for His strength to help me.

God said to Paul in II Corinthians 12:9 NIV, "My grace is sufficient for you, for My power is made perfect in weakness." Paul's response was, "Therefore I will boast all the more gladly about my weaknesses, so that Christ's power may rest on me. That is why, for Christ's sake, I delight in weaknesses, in insults, in hardships, in persecutions, in difficulties. For when I am weak, then I am strong" (II Corinthians 12:10 NIV).

Take note of everything Paul said he delights in. They are all failures. How many times have we felt so weak we felt we just had to eat something? How many times has an insult about our weight actually made us go pig out on one of our favorite desserts? When things are difficult, we tend to eat more. Many have been fired or not hired because of their weight. When any of these things happen, we turn to food. Every difficulty just makes us want to eat more.

CHAPTER 4

Paul says when we are weak, when we are failures, the Holy Spirit's power will be even more available to us. So, when we are weak, then we are strong because we are resting in God's strength and not our own.

Psalms is a great book to go to when we feel like we are failures because it tells us that God is right there to help us. "Weak and feeble ones You will sustain. Those bent over with burdens of shame You will lift up" (Psalms 145:14 TPT).

When we feel like failures, God does not leave us there. We tend to think He does, though. We think we messed up so we have to fix what's wrong, but when we try to fix things in our own strength we often make them worse. That's why I gained weight continually.

David said in Psalms 145:15-16 TPT, "You have captured our attention and the eyes of all look to You. You give what they hunger for at just the right time. When You open Your generous hand, it's full of blessings, satisfying the longings of every living thing."

FOOD DOESN'T ALWAYS MAKE US FEEL BETTER

God knows what we are hungry for and it's not something more to eat. Food is just the thing that's close at hand and what we've always used to make ourselves feel better. How much better are God's blessings of grace, mercy, comfort, and strength? These are what we really long for. He knows exactly what we need and gives it to us when we are feeling like failures.

To be successful, we have to keep trying, keep running the race, keep throwing the ball, keep going. Failure is an excuse to hide from engaging in life, but if we fail forward it can be a way for us to transform our lives. We just need to keep going.

We are not really failures until we stop. That's called quitting and that is true failure. Many times, we quit right before our breakthrough. We think we just can't take one more failure. So, we quit, but God is there encouraging us to keep trying. We just don't want to listen.

Even when we quit, God is there. Still, He is not the one condemning us. We do that ourselves. Always remember there is "no condemnation for those of us who are in Christ Jesus" (Romans 8:1 NLT). God's not sitting up in heaven wagging His finger at us or looking at us with a frown on His face. Remember, He looked down through all eternity and saw that we would fail. He knows our tendencies, but He is ready to gently pick us back up again.

> God's not sitting up in heaven wagging His finger at us or looking at us with a frown on His face.

He told us what His desires are for us in Jeremiah 29:11 NLT. "'For I know the plans I have for you,' says the Lord. 'They are plans for good and not for disaster, to give you a future and a hope.'" We may feel like our failures have resulted in disaster, but our stories are not over yet.

David felt like a failure, but he cried out to God and said, "My flesh and my heart may fail, but God is the strength of my heart and my portion" (Psalms 73:25 ESV).

Instead of staying stuck in his failure, David gave God the glory for rescuing him. "He drew me up from the pit of destruction, out of the miry bog, and set my feet upon a rock, making my steps secure. He put a new song in my mouth, a song of praise to our God. Many will see and fear, and put their trust in the Lord" (Psalm 40:2-3 ESV).

Knowing that God is there for us and will help us find our way back out of the pit of failure we have placed ourselves in is so important on our journey. He is our strength. We can lean on Him.

Many are so afraid of failure they won't even start on their healthy living journeys. This is exactly what the enemy wants. He wants us stuck in failure and despair. He is a master at trying to keep us there because he knows our tendencies are just to eat more which he wants because he knows it will eventually destroy us.

THE ENEMY'S AGENDA

We need to remember the enemy's agenda. "The thief comes only to steal and kill and destroy. I have come that they may have life, and have it to the full" (John 10:10 NIV). There is nothing more destructive than the fear of failure. It stops us in our tracks and we feel we can't go forward.

However, we don't have to use our failures as an excuse to stay stuck in the past or in one specific location. We can turn our failures into lessons that lead to our success and our growth as believers in Christ.

Many try this in their own strength and just feel more beat down. We can't do this on our own. We can only do it with God's help.

Feeling stuck is many times a product of bad habits we've adopted over the years. They could be from our family of origin. We just can't seem to force ourselves to stop baking and eating Grandma's special cake because it comforts us and makes us feel close to her.

If you only bake those things once a year it might not be that bad, but if it's something you find yourself doing all the time then you are likely stuck in a prison of your own making. The regret you feel is because you know eating that specific thing will add several pounds to your body. Instead, how about making a fresh fruit salad? Mine always has to have strawberries and pecans with other fruits thrown in.

It's hard to binge on fruit. It's better for me and more filling. If I were to eat cake, I would never get full of it and would simply keep eating. This is a disaster waiting to happen. My past failures and behaviors have taught me what not to do. In their place I've learned what works best for me.

One time I was at a conference where a friend baked some gluten-free cookies. She put a note on them so we'd know they were gluten-free. It was only me and one other person requesting gluten-free items, so I figured she made them for us. I wanted to make sure she wasn't upset if no one ate her cookies, so I took one. It was good. I went back for more and more. Full disclosure, they were not sugar-free, but still I didn't recongnize the tempter's ploy.

> **What are you doing?**

When the conference was over, I asked if there were any more. She didn't have any of those, but she had another kind with even more sugar in them. I said I wanted to take some home to my husband, but that was an excuse to eat more.

I was driving home eating a cookie and I heard God say to me, "What are you doing?" I said, "I'm throwing this cookie out the window." And I did. Then, I took the rest home and told my husband to eat them, hide them, or throw them away and not tell me where they were.

The lesson I learned that day is the enemy, who is out to do us in, will always find new ways to tempt us. This temptation was subtle. It was clothed in helping a friend feel good about her choices, even though they were not the best for me.

I learned to be vigilant, but I also learned that God is always there and will help me if I listen to Him and do what He tells me to do. "The Lord is the one who is going ahead of you. He will be with you. He won't abandon you or leave you. So don't be afraid or terrified" (Deuteronomy 31:8 ESV).

Some of us are plain scared of failure, but if we learn the lessons failure teaches us they will be with us for life. Failure is a great teacher. We just need to apply the lessons it teaches us. It will help us to grow stronger and more committed to God.

FAILURE AND DISOBEDIENCE

If our failure is a result of disobedience or sin on our part, we need to repent. David told us this in Psalms 32:3-5 NIV. "When I refused to confess my sin, my body wasted away, and I groaned all day long. Day and night Your hand of discipline was heavy on me. My strength evaporated like water in the summer heat.

"Finally, I confessed all my sins to You and stopped trying to hide my guilt. I said to myself, 'I will confess my rebellion to the Lord.' And You forgave me! All my guilt is gone."

Sometimes we refuse to confess our failures to God because we don't see them as sin. If what we are doing is disobedience to what God has told us to do, it is sin and we must confess and repent. That means we must be willing to allow God to lead us to not do that again.

CONFESSION IS GOOD FOR THE SOUL

I lived in disobedience for way too many years. It felt like my last opportunity when I finally confessed what I had done. God already knew all about it, but He still wanted me to own my sin. Then I repented. I mourned what I had done to my body. I asked Him to give me the strength and guidance to figure out how to give up sugar and then, gluten.

That's when God taught me how to change my habits and my lifestyle. I finally admitted I needed help. I knew I couldn't do this by myself. I needed a group of others like me who were on the same journey. I needed another, a mentor. More than anything I needed the Other, God Himself. I wouldn't have been successful without all these ingredients.

My coach had failed and then succeeded. All those in the group were like me and had failed and were wanting to succeed. We were not afraid to hand our failures to God and allow Him to teach us how to move forward. God is always gracious, loving and kind to help us, even in our failures.

CHAPTER 4

PRAY THIS PRAYER

"Father God, You see how I am afraid of failure. It's something we all experience every day in some form or another because none of us are perfect.

"Help me to take a step into the land of success by putting myself completely in Your hands.

"Help me to stop giving the excuse of I'll fail. Help me to be bold enough not just to try again, but to commit again and not give up.

"In Your Son's name, Amen."

ANSWER THESE QUESTIONS

1. What has been your biggest failure?

2. Have you stopped trying to lose weight because of this failure?

3. What lesson did you learn from this failure that you can take forward?

4. How has God worked through your failures to bring something good into your life?

5. Have you ever pigged out because you felt weak? Been insulted about your weight and it drove you to eat more? Turned to food in hardships and difficulties? How can you allow God to be your strength during these times?

6. Choose one of these verses and journal about it. Psalms 73:26, 40:2-3, or 145:14-16.

7. Read Psalms 32:3-5 and confess to God anything that is holding you back from losing weight.

CHAPTER 4

CHAPTER 5

I LOVE A PARTY!

I can't lose weight because I want to eat at family gatherings, parties, and holidays. When a party, holiday or family get-together happens I look forward to it. This is an excuse I hear often.

We begin thinking about seeing everyone, so our next thought is, "I need to lose weight, but this isn't the right time. I don't want to be limited in what I can eat. I want to have fun like everyone else." So, we use the thing that might have been a reason to begin losing weight to become an excuse for not losing weight.

When one woman realized she was using every event or gathering that came up as an excuse for not getting healthy, she finally drew a line in the sand.

She said, "I'm going to get healthy anyway no matter what comes along, but I can't do it without Your help, God." She made a firm decision not to let her excuses rule her and she asked for God's guidance and direction.

CHAPTER 5

I used the excuse of "I love a party" for years especially around the Christmas holiday. My year would go like this. On January 1, I would decide I have to do something about my weight. I would hunker down, muster my self-effort, and refrain from eating anything I loved. I could rally that willpower for about nine months and lose 100 pounds.

This was basically because I ate less than 1,000 calories a day, which I do not recommend for anyone, and didn't eat any sugar or bread. Then, September would come when we used to have three major family reunions. Really, who can stay on a restrictive diet when some of the best cooks in the world are bringing food to a required family event?

TOO MUCH FOOD

Right on the tails of those events came Halloween. Candy had a big pull on me, probably because of the incident with the caramels and my mother. For Halloween as an in-charge adult, I'd buy all my favorite candy. I would intentionally buy too much and eat what I wanted before, during and after Halloween.

Next came Thanksgiving and at least three family dinners during that time. I love turkey, which is a great meat to eat, low in calories, and high in protein. Unfortunately, it was accompanied by gravy, dressing, mashed potatoes, and the best homemade rolls and pecan pies around.

Then, there was Christmas and pre-Christmas parties and the ongoing Christmas treats throughout that season. I couldn't get through a Christmas without making homemade sugar cookies and my great grandma's oatmeal cake. It was one of those heavy, sugar-laden cakes that made you want more and more.

By January 1, I had put back on all the weight I had lost. The next year I'd use the excuse of dieting is just making me fatter so I'm not going to do that this year. Instead of dieting, I'd eat what I wanted, gain more weight, and go through the September to December time frame eating even more. By the next year it would feel like I had to diet or just lie down and die.

> My excuse of I have to eat because I love a party made me fatter than ever.

Where did my excuse of "I have to eat because I love a party" get me? Fatter than I had ever been. This was the endless cycle that went on year after year. I knew what I was doing, but my excuse was that I loved food. Basically, I loved a party that had great food.

Another woman said, "I don't want to hurt the feelings of the one who made the food by not eating what they fixed." I understand because I felt I had to eat what others fixed, as well. Then, I would praise them for making such wonderful foods, talk about the ingredients, and ask how they made it taste so good. I loved to see them beam from ear to ear with the compliments I gave.

Actually, I complimented them so next year they would be sure to bring that great dessert or dish again. This really backfired on me when I started on my healthy living journey. People were always making my favorite dishes and then wondering why I wasn't eating them. This was especially true

CHAPTER 5

of desserts because those were the ones I had praised the most before going on my healthy living journey.

They would dish up my favorite dessert and bring it to me when they noticed I wasn't eating any. When I'd tell them I was full, they didn't believe me because I'd always eaten it in the past. They would seem sad that they couldn't please me. Then I noticed that no one pushed desserts on my husband. That's because he rarely eats dessert. If he does, it is a small portion.

LYING ABOUT NOT WANTING DESSERT

At the start of my transformation journey I was lying when I said I was full, or I didn't want any because neither thing was true. I still wanted the desserts; I was just committed to God's admonition of not eating sugar. It was a while, though, before I could give that answer.

After losing a substantial amount of weight, I got the courage to tell people what I was really doing. I'd explain that I am fasting sugar and flour for the rest of my life in order to stay healthy and that I am doing this to honor God. They'd usually ask how much I'd lost, and I'd tell them. It wasn't until I'd lost over 100 pounds before I felt secure enough to share the truth. Close family knew, but I felt everyone else was just waiting for me to fail.

Before, I didn't want to tell them about my new way of eating because I might start gaining weight again like I always had before. It would make me look like a fool and I would have failed God who was being the strength to take me on this crazy journey. Who fasts sugar and flour for the rest of their lives? I do because God told me to.

I used those thoughts that could have stopped me in my tracks to propel me forward to be an example of what a person can achieve when they focus on God and His strength instead of the foods they think they can't live without. By that time, I had realized not only can I live without what were my favorite foods, but I don't want them anymore.

These days one of the biggest questions I get is if I am ever tempted to eat sugar. I am finally far enough along on my journey that I do not even want to eat what is sweet. It's no longer something I desire. That much sweetness would make me sick today.

The other thing people ask is, "If God really has helped you on your journey, shouldn't you be able to eat a little sugar and not go hog-wild?" My answer is, "Would you say that to an alcoholic? Would you tell her that she should be able to drink a little alcohol? I am a sugar addict. I can't eat a little sugar and stop."

> I am a sugar addict. I can't eat a little sugar and stop.

I don't understand the physiology of it, but there are a lot of people who can drink a little alcohol and stop. Then there are those who put others' lives in danger by driving drunk and not even being aware of what they are doing.

Sugar doesn't endanger others' lives in the same way. It does, however, endanger those prone to continuing to binge on it because it can lead to severe obesity and many diseases. It also endangers others' lives when we cook that way and they eat what we've cooked. I don't know which person or child is or will become a sugar addict so I cook healthy. It is one way I can show love to those I love.

CHAPTER 5

Since sugar is very addictive to me, I have agreed with God that I should not eat it. However, I also know what God told Noah in Genesis 9:4 NLT. "All living creatures are yours for food; just as I gave you the plants, now I give you everything else."

Paul gave more instruction regarding foods in Romans 14:14 NLT. "I know and am convinced on the authority of the Lord Jesus that no food, in and of itself, is wrong to eat. But if someone believes it is wrong, then for that person it is wrong."

That discussion started with what Paul said in Romans 14:1-3 NLT, "Accept other believers who are weak in faith, and don't argue with them about what they think is right or wrong. For instance, one person believes it's all right to eat anything. But another believer with a sensitive conscience will eat only vegetables. Those who feel free to eat anything must not look down on those who don't. And those who don't eat certain foods must not condemn those who do, for God has accepted them."

These verses all taken together tell us all foods, plant- and animal-based, are alright for believers to eat. Paul especially defers to the conscience or the convictions of individual believers as their guides for what they should and should not eat.

GOD'S PERSONALIZED EATING PLAN

Eating decisions depend on whether or not we have a firm word from God. I did and I ignored it for years. As I look back on my life, I see the myriad of excuses I used in order to not follow what God clearly told me to do. I do want to emphasize the word "me" because it is a decision that each believer must make. What I teach in Overcomers Academy is not a diet or even how to stop eating sugar. I help those who have a problem with food determine if they are an overeater, binge eater, or sugar addict.

Once we know what tendencies we have, we can develop a lifestyle eating plan with God's help. We can see where we need to place limits and boundaries on certain foods and agree to go with unlimited amounts of things like water and exercise. We can learn from all the diets we have been on in the past what pieces of each plan God might show us should go in our personalized forever plans.

No two lifestyle change plans will be alike. I am very different in that I do not expect your plan to look like mine because you are not me. God made us all different. One reason He did is so we will come to Him for the help we need.

> No two lifestyle change plans will be alike.

We may have all been spending a crazy amount of money on diets, diet plans, diet drinks, diet foods, and yet we are still overweight. We need to go to God, surrender our issues to Him and ask for His help and strength to do what He tells us to do.

Paul had quite a bit of advice about food. He chastises the Corinthian church about how they have been desecrating the Lord's Supper. Back then it wasn't just a sip of juice and a piece of cracker. It had become what we might consider a church potluck dinner and Paul was not happy with what was going on.

"You come together, and instead of eating the Lord's Supper, you bring in a lot of food from the outside and make pigs of yourselves. Some are left out, and go home hungry. Others have to be carried out, too drunk to walk. I can't believe it! Don't you have your own homes to eat and drink in? Why would you stoop to desecrating God's church? Why would you actually shame God's poor? I never would have believed you would stoop to this. And I'm not going to stand by and say nothing" (1 Corinthians 11:20-22 MSG).

NOT FOR SELF-INDULGENCE

What Paul is talking about is self-indulgence at the expense of the purpose of the Lord's Supper. He said, "If you're so hungry that you can't wait to be served, go home and get a sandwich. But by no means risk turning this meal into an eating and drinking binge or a family squabble. It is a spiritual meal—a love feast" (1 Corinthians 11:34 MSG).

He also reminded them of the original purpose of the Lord's Supper. "You must solemnly realize that every time you eat this bread and every time you drink this cup, you reenact in your words and actions the death of the Master. You will be drawn back to this meal again and again until the Master returns. You must never let familiarity breed contempt" (1 Corinthians 11:25-26 MSG).

The English Standard Version of this verse says, "For every time you eat this bread and drink this cup, you are proclaiming the Lord's death until He comes." This version emphasizes the spiritual importance of the Lord's Supper.

Paul had just cautioned them about what they had been doing by gorging themselves on food and drink and now, in essence, he told them to treat the Lord's Supper like Jesus is sitting right there with them.

For the people of that day, bread and wine was what was available at every meal. So when Jesus said every time you eat this bread and drink this cup, He meant every time, three meals a day. They were to constantly be reminding themselves of Jesus' spilled blood and body broken for them.

Of course, there are special set aside times called the Lord's Supper, but it strikes me that Jesus took ordinary table food and told the people every time you eat, remember Me. What if every time we sat down to eat a meal and drink a glass of water, we remembered Jesus blood and body? It certainly makes me pause and think about what He did for me.

Romans 14:17 NLT has the very best advice. "For the Kingdom of God is not a matter of what we eat or drink, but of living a life of goodness and peace and joy in the Holy Spirit." Those in the Corinthians church were arguing about what they could eat and couldn't eat. Paul tells them that's not important at all. What's important is living the right kind of life.

HOW TO HANDLE CARRY-IN DINNERS

They were indulging themselves in food too much and making a mockery out of the Lord's Supper. Both were wrong, but it's interesting that they both were about food and a party, even if they were church parties.

It is so true that we love a great church carry-in dinner with all the home-made foods, right? The first time I went to a carry-in dinner after I started my lifestyle change, I decided to do things differently. Instead of going through the line to get

CHAPTER 5

food, I went around to tables and sat and talked with people while they were eating. I had a general kind of question to ask like, "What's new in your life?"

I enjoyed the fellowship. Isn't that what we are supposed to do at a party? It's not supposed to be about the food. It's supposed to be a time to enjoy each other. We can do the same thing with family and friends.

When I'm going to a party of any kind, I take a dish that is something I can eat. My go-to is a fresh fruit salad with pecans and/or a grilled chicken salad. Both of these are likely to be consumed by others, so I make sure I set some aside for myself ahead of time. It helps me to not get caught being ravenous and eating something I shouldn't.

> I want to be a witness for my God and eating healthy is one way I can do that.

The other thing that helps me is to remember I have told people about my journey and God is leading me. I want to be a good example whether I am at a restaurant, friend's house, church gathering, or my own home. Because of the stand I have taken, I am aware people are watching what I am eating. I want to be a witness for my God and eating healthy is one way I can do that.

The King James Version of Romans 14:17 is what I want us to remember. "For the kingdom of God is not meat and drink; but righteousness, and peace, and joy in the Holy Ghost."

No food holds a candle to righteousness, peace, and joy in the Holy Ghost!

PRAY THIS PRAYER

"Jesus, I love You. Thank You for what You did on the cross for me.

"You poured out Your blood for me. You allowed Your body to be broken for me. You died for me and then rose again to take away my sins.

"Help me understand that eating all the food I can stomach is not the ultimate goal You have for me. You died for me to live a righteous life, to have peace, and to enjoy the precious Holy Spirit.

"Help me make that be my goal. In Your Name I pray. Amen."

ANSWER THESE QUESTIONS

1. When you are invited to someone's house for dinner and they serve things that are not on your eating plan, what do you do?

2. Is there a specific holiday or party where you know you will be tempted to eat outside of your boundaries? What can you do about that?

CHAPTER 5

3. How can you focus on the people rather than the food at a gathering of family and friends?

4. Why is it important to eat within your boundaries even though it is a special occasion?

5. How can what you eat be a witness to others? Journal about that.

6. Have you ever gone to a church dinner and acted even remotely like what was happening in 1 Cor. 11:20-22 MSG?

7. What would it mean to your life to really follow what it says in Romans 14:17 KJV?

I LOVE A PARTY!

CHAPTER 5

*"For the kingdom of God
is not meat and drink;
but righteousness,
and peace, and joy in
the Holy Ghost."*

ROMANS 14:17 KJV

CHAPTER 6

I CAN'T LOSE WEIGHT

I can't. Those two words should be erased from our vocabularies because they are an excuse that keeps us stuck. This is true whether it is trying to change a flat tire, balancing a budget, forgiving a spouse, or losing weight. If we start with the excuse of I can't, then where else is there to go? We've just slammed the door on any forward motion.

Years ago, I was somewhere out in the boondocks on a gravel road and had a flat tire. This was before cell phones. I was a teenager just learning to drive and my dad had showed me how to change a tire, but I had never done it myself.

My first thought was, I can't change this tire. I don't even know if I have a spare or where the jack is. I don't remember how to change a tire. I've never changed a tire before. What if I can't do it and I'm stuck out here forever? I was holding a big-time pity party. Truth was, I just didn't want to get all dirty and muggy in the heat. So, I told myself I can't.

Finally, though, I realized I was on a country road where very few people travel and if I didn't at least try to figure out how to change the tire, I'd be there all night and the next day. I managed to find the spare and all the parts and I changed that obstinate tire. I did what I was sure I couldn't do. I changed a tire.

This might not seem like an insurmountable task, but for me at the time it was. It wasn't easy and it wasn't fun. However, the satisfaction of getting that task done was better than getting straight A's in second grade, which was a real high point in my life.

I DON'T WANT TO

It really wasn't that I couldn't change a tire. It was I didn't want to change a tire. I think we do the same thing with the excuse of I can't lose weight. It's not so much we can't as it is that we don't want to.

I get it. I really do. Losing weight and keeping it off is not easy. It's difficult and for some it feels impossible. However, the statement of I can't lose weight, at least for me, was just an excuse. It was not the truth.

When I was super, morbidly obese, I thought I couldn't lose weight because I had been on so many diets. Any diet that came along I'd try. Some didn't work for me at all. A few worked for me to lose weight, but I couldn't keep it off because my craving for sugar would always kick in when I reached a goal and felt I needed a reward for a job well done. Indulging again just propelled me towards gaining weight again because I would just go back to eating what I wanted.

I was tired of diets, even tired of Christian-based programs. None of the ones I tried worked because they were all just other diets. They didn't address the core issue of why I was overeating in the first place. I figured I was too far gone and that no one could help me with the level of food issues I had. I didn't understand then that I was a sugar addict. I just thought I loved food. Didn't everybody? Why can some people eat sugar and not gain weight? If I just look at sugar.I seemed to gain several pounds?

If I wanted to eat desserts, I would eat them nonstop until I was satisfied, but I was never satisfied. The devil had me right between the crosshairs and his hand was on the trigger. It's extremely scary for me to say this, but I know the evil one wanted me gone and was doing a good job of causing it to happen. At one point in my life, I actually thought if I couldn't eat foods made with sugar and flour I didn't want to live, but I also didn't want to live at the weight I was. I was stuck.

> The evil one wanted me gone and was doing a good job of causing it to happen.

I know many are at various weights. Some may only have 30 pounds to lose, while some have over 300 pounds to lose. Both can feel like impossible tasks when we've tried and failed to keep the weight off. Both can be extremely dangerous territories for various diseases to take root if we don't lose the weight and keep it off.

The sad truth is being obese, morbidly obese, and especially super morbidly obese can kill you. At one time I felt like I would take that chance if I could just keep eating what I wanted to eat. I felt like I couldn't lose weight if it meant I could no longer eat foods made with sugar. I would rather die.

CHAPTER 6

A woman I know and love passed away due to heart issues, which resulted from the amount of weight she carried. She had wanted to lose weight and in the last year of her life had begun to do that, but it was too late. I mourn her passing because she was such a bright light on this earth. We all have a destiny and hers was cut way too short.

The devil's agenda is to destroy us any way he can. He knows what God can do with us when we break free of food addiction and begin to help others. So he tries everything he can to keep us in bondage to the foods we love. I hate the fact that I actually allowed food to control me. It became my god because I wanted it more than I wanted God's presence in my life.

WHY EVERYTHING CHANGED

Everything changed when my mentor said, "Alcohol is one molecule away from sugar. Alcohol is liquid sugar." His statement hit me like a ton of bricks because my dad's side of the family was comprised of many alcoholics.

When I was a kid, I asked my dad about a neighbor who was doing some crazy things to his wife that my little brother and I witnessed. I asked, "Why was he being so mean? He's usually so nice."

Dad said, "He's a great guy, but he is an alcoholic. When he drinks, he doesn't know what he is doing."

Then Dad asked me to promise I would never drink alcohol or become addicted. I am not an alcohol drinker, but I realized after hearing what my mentor said that I was like an alcoholic, only with sugar. Since I'd never heard of sugar addiction I asked him, "Can a person be addicted to sugar?"

He said, "You can be addicted to anything that controls you." That was it for me. I knew I was a sugar addict because sugar controlled me.

Paul described what I had to do in Ephesians 4:22-24 TPT. "Let go of the lifestyle of the ancient man, the old self-life, which was corrupted by sinful and deceitful desires that spring from delusions.

"Now it's time to be made new by every revelation that's been given to you. And to be transformed as you embrace the glorious Christ-within as your new life and live in union with Him! For God has re-created you all over again in His perfect righteousness, and you now belong to Him in the realm of true holiness."

> I had to figure out how to give up sugar for the rest of my life.

I had to figure out how to give up sugar for the rest of my life. God had told me that years ago, but I was sure I couldn't live without it. Basically, I was saying I can't give up sugar. No way. No how. I'll die without it.

However, I had finally come to the end of my rope. I had exhausted all my efforts to lose weight. I decided, "I can't lose weight. So, I'm not even going to try." That's when God saw I was ready to do things His way. I was ready to handle more of His truth. He revealed to me that I am a sugar addict. I hadn't honored Dad's request. I had become an addict.

I have come to see when God gives us a directive, guidance, or plan and we don't understand why or how to implement it, we only need to ask Him, and He will tell us. He will let us know.

Nearly every week when we do our Overcomers Academy calls, or when I am on a one-on-one freedom coaching call, I do what I call God Connection. We identify a lie that a person is believing about God. For example, the Holy Spirit won't comfort me, so I have to comfort myself. Then, we have a conversation to get to the root of why the individual believes that lie.

GETTING TO THE ROOT

One woman told me that God had been showing her a certain situation where she got physically hurt as a child, but it upset her mother so she, as the child, became the comforter instead of her mother.

God was showing her she couldn't accept the comfort of the Holy Spirit because as a child she had the idea that she had to figure out how to comfort herself. We went through the process of forgiving her mother and renouncing the lie that the Holy Spirit would treat her the same way. Then, she asked God, "What is Your truth?" Every time we do this, God answers each person in a different way.

She saw a picture of God's arms wrapping her in comfort. As she saw the picture, she cried tears of joy as she literally felt that comfort while we were talking. She rationally knew the Holy Spirit is the Comforter, but she didn't feel He was comforting her. So, when she would need comfort, she felt she had to comfort herself with food.

Jesus said in John 8:32 NIV, "You will know the truth and the truth will set you free." In the Message version that same verse says, "You will experience the truth and truth will free you." What this woman experienced was the freedom of God's truth. Experience is so much deeper than just knowledge. It leads to the truth that we can lose weight if we follow the boundaries God reveals to us.

The excuse of I can't lose weight is one we use mainly out of fear. We are afraid we will fail again and then we will be a multiple failure. None of us is perfect. We are all humans. We will fail. However, when we quit and we don't even try, we have ceased to want anything more for ourselves.

This earth is just a training ground. We are here to learn more about how to navigate life in this flesh-suit. It is specially designed to fail at certain times, and we have to learn how to trust God to get us through those times of testing and trials.

The only way to make it through is to rely on His strength and ability to direct us. If we try to figure it out on our own, we will certainly fail. However, when we trust God to show us what to do everything might not be the way we want it to be, but we will be following Him. Throughout all eternity, that's all that matters.

SEVEN STEPS OUT OF THE I CAN'T LIFESTYLE

If you are willing to step out and try again, if you are willing to lay aside the idea that you can't, then I've got seven steps out of the "I can't" lifestyle.

First, God loves us just as we are. He sees us as beautiful. After all, He created us.

CHAPTER 6

"You made all the delicate inner parts of my body and knit me together in my mother's womb ... You watched me as I was being formed in utter seclusion, as I was woven together in the dark of the womb. You saw me before I was born. Every day of my life was recorded in Your book. Every moment was laid out before a single day had passed" (Psalms 139:13, 15-16 TPT).

"Don't be concerned about the outward beauty that depends on jewelry, or beautiful clothes, or hair arrangement. Be beautiful inside, in your hearts, with the lasting charm of a gentle and quiet spirit that is so precious to God. That kind of deep beauty was seen in the saintly women of old, who trusted God and fitted in with their husbands' plans." (1 Peter 3:3-5 TLB).

> God wants us to honor Him with our bodies.

Second, God wants us to honor Him with our bodies. That means not doing anything that harms our bodies. Overeating is a way we dishonor our bodies. God calls it gluttony. I'm sorry, but that is just the truth.

"Don't you realize that your body is the temple of the Holy Spirit, who lives in you and was given to you by God? You do not belong to yourself, for God bought you with a high price. So you must honor God with your body" (I Corinthians 6:19-20 NLT).

"Those who belong to Christ Jesus have nailed the passions and desires of their sinful nature to His cross and crucified them there. Since we are living by the Spirit, let us follow the Spirit's leading in every part of our lives" (Galatians 5:24-25 NLT).

Third, God doesn't condemn us for what we have done to ourselves. "Now there is no condemnation for those who belong to Christ Jesus" (Romans 8:1 NLT).

"With the arrival of Jesus, the Messiah, that fateful dilemma is resolved. Those who enter into Christ's being-here-for-us no longer have to live under a continuous, low-lying black cloud. A new power is in operation.

"The Spirit of life in Christ, like a strong wind, has magnificently cleared the air, freeing you from a fated lifetime of brutal tyranny at the hands of sin and death" (Romans 8:1-2 MSG).

Fourth, in order to allow God to work in our lives we must confess what we have done, repent and ask Him to give us strength and direction for how to go forward on our journeys.

> Surrender completely to God in order to be transformed into the person He wants you to be.

"If we claim we have no sin, we are only fooling ourselves and not living in the truth. But if we confess our sins to Him, He is faithful and just to forgive us our sins and to cleanse us from all wickedness" (I John 1:8-9 NLT).

"God, give me mercy from Your fountain of forgiveness! I know Your abundant love is enough to wash away my guilt. Because Your compassion is so great, take away this shameful guilt of sin. Forgive the full extent of my rebellious ways and erase this deep stain on my conscience" (Psalms 51:1 TPT).

Fifth, surrender completely to God in order to be transformed into the person He wants you to become. Surrender is not a one-time event. It is a daily process to stay in tune with what God desires for you.

CHAPTER 6

"I urge you, brothers and sisters, in view of God's mercy, to offer your bodies as a living sacrifice, holy and pleasing to God—this is your true and proper worship. Do not conform to the pattern of this world, but be transformed by the renewing of your mind. Then you will be able to test and approve what God's will is—His good, pleasing and perfect will" (Romans 12:1-2 NIV).

> Experience breakthrough as you follow God.

"Don't give up; don't be impatient; be entwined as one with the Lord. Be brave and courageous, and never lose hope. Yes, keep on waiting—for He will never disappoint you!" (Psalms 27:14 TPT).

Sixth, experience breakthrough as you follow God and allow Him to hold you close.

"Let my passion for life be restored, tasting joy in every breakthrough You bring to me. Hold me close to You with a willing spirit that obeys whatever You say" (Psalms 51:12 TPT).

"Your forgiving love is what makes You so wonderful. No wonder You are loved and worshiped! This is why I wait upon You, expecting Your breakthrough, for Your Word brings me hope" (Psalms 130:4-5 TPT).

Seventh, don't try to do everything on your own. Ask God to give you strength and allow Him to do it.

"Trust God from the bottom of your heart; don't try to figure out everything on your own. Listen for God's voice in everything you do, everywhere you go. He's the one who will keep you on track. Don't assume that you know it all. Run to God! Run from evil! Your body will glow with health, your very bones will vibrate with life!" (Proverbs 3:5-7 MSG).

"So, here's what I've learned through it all: Leave all your cares and anxieties at the feet of the Lord, and measureless grace will strengthen you" (Psalms 55:22 TPT).

I know from personal experience that losing weight and keeping it off is hard, but it is not impossible. If I can do it, you can do it, but we need His strength. We must always go to Him no matter what is happening. There will be hard times because God has not promised us a pain-free existence.

When you feel like you can't go on because your strength is gone, remember where your strength comes from. "When you abide under the shadow of Shaddai, you are hidden in the strength of God Most High. He's the hope that holds me and the stronghold to shelter me, the only God for me, and my great confidence" (Psalms 91:1-2 TPT).

> With God all things are possible.

It is true that we can't lose weight on our own. We can, though, with God's help and strength. When I started my transformation journey, I was convinced I couldn't lose weight. I couldn't be myself unless I ate the foods I loved. I couldn't exist without those foods. I said to myself, "I can't lose weight and keep it off. I can't. I can't. I can't."

Then God stepped in and said, "I know you can't do this on your own. Let Me help you. You can do this with My guidance and My strength. All things are possible with Me." And that made all the difference in the world.

What He did for me, He will do for you if you want Him to. If you are committed to Him.

CHAPTER 6

PRAY THIS PRAYER

"Dear Lord Jesus, I am weary of trying to lose weight in my own strength and power, trying to find the right plan, trying, trying, trying. It has me to the point where I think I am doomed and can't lose weight.

"Give me hope, Lord. Give me strength. Give me power to overcome my cravings. Help me crave only You and what You want for me.

"I am down. Pick me up. Revive me. Refresh me. Renew me and point me in the right direction.

"In Your name, I pray. Amen."

ANSWER THESE QUESTIONS

1. To step out of the "I can't" lifestyle you first need to see yourself the way God sees you. How does God see you?

2. God wants you to honor Him with your body. What is one thing you can change today to begin in order to do that?

3. God doesn't condemn you, but do you condemn yourself? Be honest.

4. The fourth step is to confess what you have done, repent, and ask God to give you the strength to go forward. Write a prayer doing that right now.

5. To transform, you must surrender completely to God. Write a heartfelt prayer of surrender to Him.

6. Breakthrough comes when you follow God and allow Him to hold you close. Envision Him doing that right now. Ask Him, what do You think of me? Write out what He says.

7. Trying to change the way you eat on your own hasn't worked. Ask Him to give you strength to do what you couldn't do one second before. Ask Him for specifics and write down what He says.

: CHAPTER 6

CHAPTER 7

FEAR OF SUCCESS

There is a fear that can keep us stuck. It is a fear the enemy loves to keep hidden from us. It is the fear of success. We are afraid of moving forward because we might succeed and then we will have to continue the hard work that we think success will take. We are afraid of what success might do to us and how it will change us.

Since I have been coaching literally thousands have come through my coaching groups, courses, and free programs. Many have lost weight and kept it off. Others, though, have left because they finally understood the level of commitment they needed to lose weight and keep it off. They were unwilling to commit to do the work.

They left without getting what they needed because some said, "That's great for you. You must just be special because I could never do that. I could never give up sugar." I thought the same thing, but it was fear of being without my crutch that kept me stuck for way too many years.

CHAPTER 7

Most of us want a quick fix. We don't want to put in the time and effort it takes to change our ingrown habits. So far no one I know of has successfully invented something that makes us lose weight and keep it off without any work. It didn't take us a day to gain weight and it will not come off in a day.

Any kind of success is going to take hard work to maintain. However, it will be made easier by surrendering completely to God. Surrender is another hard issue we have difficulty with. That's probably because we also have control issues. We don't want to turn over the control of our food to God. We see it as the last thing we have control over.

I'll be honest. I never had real control over what I ate. My kind of control gave me carte blanche to eat whatever I wanted. I was in control of pigging out, but I was definitely not in control of food. Food was in control of me.

Surrendering control of what I eat to God was the best thing I ever did. Listening to His advice on every aspect of my life has made me realize how out of control I was. I do understand the excuse of I can't surrender to God because I have to be in control of what I eat. However, trying to be in control is what got us in this place to begin with.

GRACE AND COMPASSION

God called me to coach and God gifted me with the missing ingredient I didn't even know I needed. I asked Him how can I coach people? I know all the excuses because I have used them all myself. He told me, "You do it like I did with you. You do it with grace and compassion." I knew I had His grace, which is more than His gift of salvation. It's also His power to do what I couldn't do one second before.

I remember very vividly this talk with God because I saw all the times I told Him I was going to lose weight, always by dieting so I could get it done quickly with the intent of going back to eating all my favorite foods.

Not once did He chastise me, but He let me experience my success of losing weight followed by my despair when I then started eating my favorite foods and gained all the weight back plus more. He did not condemn me.

He kept calling me back to the initial plan He had given me of giving up sugar. He knew there would come a time when I would come to the end of my self-imposed frustrations. Then, He knew I would come back to Him, and He would show me my way was not the right approach.

> He knew I would come back to Him and He would show me my way was not the right approach.

I didn't have the compassion and patience that God had. If I was going to coach, I knew I needed both of those. I admitted that to Him and He said, "You have it now." He gave me compassion and patience because He knew I would need it for the next leg of my journey.

One of my favorite verses about the compassion of God declared, "'Though the mountains be shaken and the hills be removed, yet My unfailing love for you will not be shaken nor My covenant of peace be removed,' says the Lord who has compassion on you" (Isaiah 54:10 NIV).

CHAPTER 7

When God showed me these next verses, I understood why I needed compassion. "Praise be to the God and Father of our Lord Jesus Christ, the Father of compassion and the God of all comfort, who comforts us in all our troubles, so that we can comfort those in any trouble with the comfort we ourselves receive from God" (2 Cor. 1:3-4 NIV).

COMPASSION CAN BE PAINFUL

We have compassion from God so that we can pass it on to others. One of my favorite things to do in my coaching group is help individuals through a process where we work with God to discover the core issues holding them back.

Those times are always highlights for me, but then my compassion also becomes a deep pain when people just don't get it. God modeled His compassion to me by letting me continue doing what I wanted to do until I finally came to the end of my resources.

I have to allow others to do that, too. I can't force anyone to do something they don't want to do. If they don't want to surrender to God, I can't make them. I can only share with them the extreme difference submission to God made in my life. They have their excuses as to why they can't surrender. I just have to wait them out. That's where patience comes in.

What is so awesome to me is when someone who has been in our group for a long time, finally gets over their fear of success and starts down the right path. I don't know why it takes some longer, but I am so happy that God gave me the patience to wait knowing that the breakthrough wss just around the corner.

When I first started coaching there was a woman who didn't want to share and was really closed about her life. I wasn't sure why she was in the group except she was very overweight and said she wanted to stop the control food had on her. The control was strong. I prayed for her daily.

She wanted to continue to be a victim. If she never reached for success, she could stay sad, lonely, and depressed. At least it wouldn't take any effort on her part. Her issue was fear of success and fear of what change might do to her. She also had a fear of Jesus, even though she had invited Him into her heart, and she was afraid of others.

During this time, God gave me the following story to help her, and others understand how desperately God wants to move us from fear into success.

OUT OF FEAR INTO SUCCESS

There used to be a room in her house which was extremely comfortable and cozy. All the chairs were soft recliners and couches she could sink into. The carpet was thick and soft. It just begged to be walked across bare-footed.

In this room, she had everything she wanted within arm's reach—her favorite snacks and foods and cold beverages. More than that when she was in this room, she could eat whatever she wanted and it not affect her health, at least that's what she told herself.

She could lounge around in her most comfortable clothes and relax watching movies on the big screen television that covered the wall. Everything in her room seemed to ease any anxiety or stress she had.

CHAPTER 7

She could invite friends and family into this room if she wanted, but only when she wanted company. The door had no handle on the outside and was invisible to anyone walking by.

She had to open the door for anyone to come inside, but she had never wanted to share her private space with anyone else.

One day someone knocked on the door. Since this rarely happened, she asked, "Who is it?"

On the other side of the door, she heard a man say, "This is the opportunity of a lifetime." Then he proceeded to define for her the dream she had for herself. She knew it well. It had resided in her heart since childhood.

His last statement was, "In order to take advantage of this opportunity, you must open the door and never return to the room you are in. I will return for your answer."

> Any kind of change would be difficult, but changing her entire lifestyle distressed her greatly.

She wondered how he knew to knock on the door that no one could see from the outside—a puzzlement for sure.

She loved her room. It was perfectly set up for everything she craved, but she knew she was still not living her true dream. This brought her to the most difficult of her ponderings. To take advantage of the offer, to live her dream, she knew beyond a shadow of a doubt, she would have to succeed. That would mean she would have to change.

Any kind of change would be difficult but faced with leaving her room and changing her entire lifestyle, the one she had spent a lifetime creating, distressed her greatly.

FEAR OF SUCCEES

It would mean success, which scared her. It would mean thinking about everything she did, what she ate, what she drank, how she moved, how she managed her time, how she connected with people, how she connected with God.

Ah, God. He was someone she had not invited to her room for a long time. She just assumed He was fine staying away.

She was ashamed of what she had let her life become. She was like a big, soft mattress that just laid around and existed. Nothing moved her. Nothing.

Why would God want to visit her anyway? Letting Him in would rock her boat too much and if it rocked, she would surely drown.

Besides, even though the handle was on her side of the door, she could not open it if she tried. One day she had attempted to, but the force keeping it shut was way too strong, which was just fine with her. In the end, she decided her room was where she belonged.

> Why would God want to visit her anyway?

In her room, she had everything she needed. She told herself she was just fine.

Yet "fine" is a relative term. "How are you?" "I am fine," but she would be lying. She was not fine. She was slowly dying.

Death and life are in the power of the tongue[1] and the power of her thoughts, which leads to action or no action, success or no success. She knew this and knew her thoughts were leading her increasingly towards a slow death.

"If I've got to die someday anyway, I might as well go fat and happy," she told herself. The trouble was she wasn't happy. She

CHAPTER 7

knew there were gifts placed inside her by ... by God, whom she had left out of any decisions of major importance—decisions that were affecting her life. Decisions like what she ate. How she moved. Who she interacted with.

Fear was raging inside her. Could she leave everything she knew and loved for a life that seemed difficult, impossible, and scary?

> Could she leave everything she knew and loved for a life that seemed difficult, impossible and scary?

She looked at the door. What would it take to simply open the door? What was the force that held it closed so firmly?

She had not spoken in this room, because her thoughts resided here. Spoken words were not necessary. Maybe, though, that's what she needed now.

"God, if You're there, tell me what force holds this door closed."

He did not speak verbally, but in her heart she instantly knew. It coursed through her body like a million daggers. It was fear of success.

Could she succeed outside of what she had always known? Could she lay down the thoughts and actions that were slowly killing her?

Could she move outside her comfort zone? Could she do it if on the other side of the door of fear was life and reality and dreams fulfilled. Could she? This feeling of despair engulfed her. Moving outside all that was familiar and comfortable, her own thoughts, and creations, felt impossible.

It felt as if changing her lifestyle would be changing her identity. Yet who was she really? Was she what she did? Was she all the hats she wore? Was she the things she craved, cooked, and ate?

"Maybe it's as simple as being me," she said to herself. "Yet who am I really? Will I even like the real me?"

And therein was the fear. When she thought about stepping outside the room, she felt naked, exposed, vulnerable. To go for her dreams felt way too scary.

She might fail. She might fall flat on her face like she always had any time she had tried to be successful.

"And yet, I am dying here," she said out loud.

> It felt as if changing her lifestyle would be changing her identity.

The knock on the door was soft, but she knew it was Him.

"I am here," she said.

"Are you ready to open the door?" He asked.

She tried to turn the handle, but it would not budge. "I am trying, but the force preventing it from opening is too strong. I cannot do it!" She sank to the floor and sobbed.

"Do you want Me to come in?" His voice was soft and soothing.

"Yes."

And instantly He was there with her, in her room, the room where no one had ever been before. The room she was afraid to open to anyone.

CHAPTER 7

She looked into His eyes and without speaking told Him she was sorry for all the times she'd been afraid of Him and stayed away from Him.

Instantly, she knew all was forgiven.

"Are you ready to go?" He asked.

"How do I get out of this room?" She stood staring at the door.

"I am the Door,"[2] He said as He stepped in front of the door of fear. "I am the Door. All you need to do is go through Me and you will have abundant life[3] beyond what you can imagine."

> By faith, she walked up to Him, through grace and out into the world.

By faith, she walked up to Him, through grace[3] and out into the world.

On the other side were all of the changes she knew would be there and though she felt some anxious thoughts for a moment, she continued walking.

In a second, He was by her side.

"I'm so glad You are here. I was afraid I had to do this alone," she said.

"If there's one thing you should remember and never forget, I am with you always.[4] I will be Your guide through this life if you will let Me, if you will listen to Me and follow My voice."

"How will I know it's You?" she asked.

"You will know. You are in my fold now. Those in My flock recognize My voice and follow it.[5]

"You will not always see Me, but I am always here. Call to Me and I will answer and tell you remarkable secrets you do not know.⁶ I will guide you and be the voice saying, 'Wait. This is the path over here. Walk here if you wander off and head the wrong way.'"⁷

"And what if I get afraid again?" Her voice was soft and low.

"Then you come to Me again and ask forgiveness. You need not fear anything you've done or will do. My grace covers it all.⁸ Perfect love expels all fear.⁹ If you are afraid, it is for fear of condemnation, but I promise that I will never condemn you.¹⁰

"You need not fear because you know and have experienced the Truth which sets you free.¹¹ I've prepared the way for you. All you need to do is walk in it. Move forward. Listen to My voice. I am with you."

> You need not fear anything you've done or will do. My grace covers it all.

As she took a step and then another, she saw the beauty around her. There was the laughter from children, the blue sky, the trees, the clouds, the flowers. She saw opportunities to live and have purpose.

Her heart filled with gratitude for the One who took time to come to her, reach out to her and invite her to take that first risky step of faith.

Her life was whole. There were no more rooms of comfort behind locked doors of fear. She had begun to live. She would never be the same again.

CHAPTER 7

What's in your room of comfort that keeps you shut away from others and God? God doesn't want you to stay in your room behind your locked door. More than anything, both He and I want freedom for you.

PRAY THIS PRAYER

"Dear Jesus, I am afraid of success. I am stuck in a room of my own making. It seems comfortable, but it allows me to do whatever I want whenever I want.

"I thought I was happy, but now I realize I am not. I am a prisoner.

"More than anything, I want to be free from this bondage I have created.

"I need You, Jesus. I want You, Jesus.

"I surrender completely to You, Jesus.

"Rescue me from this hell of my own making. And I will follow You.

"In Your name. Amen."

ANSWER THESE QUESTIONS

1. Do you feel like you are afraid of success on your weight loss journey? If so, why?

2. Do you have control issues regarding surrendering your food to God? Write a sentence about how that affects your life.

3. Why do we need compassion? See 2 Corinthians 1:3-4.

4. Why was the woman in the story staying in the room of isolation? Why would you stay there? Are you there now?

5. Why do you think the woman in the story finally desired to get out of the room?

6. Do you think the woman will continue to rely on Jesus? Why or why not?

7. How does this story relate to you?

CHAPTER 7

ENDNOTES
1. Proverbs 18:21 ESV
2. John 10:9 NKJV
3. Ephesians 2:8-9 ESV
4. Matthew 28:20 ESV
5. John 10:27 ESV
6. Jeremiah 33:3 NLT
7. Isaiah 30:21 NLT
8. Ephesians 1:7-8 CEB
9. 1 John 4:18 ESV
10. Romans 8:1 NIV
11. John 8:32 MSG

CHAPTER 8

FOOD KEEPS ME SANE

Food keeps me sane was my excuse for continuing to indulge in the foods I loved the most. This was because most of my life I tried to avoid one thing—being insane like my mother was for most of my growing up years.

When I was a child until the time I went to college, my mother had emotional issues and saw a psychiatrist regularly. She was on medication, which only seemed to make her mood swings worse. She had high highs and low lows.

I never knew what kind of mother I would come home to after school. Would she be doing the jitterbug in the kitchen while fixing supper? Or would she be sitting catatonic in the living room staring into space, so unresponsive I would check to make sure she was breathing?

I became adept at sensing her moods. If I came in the house and sensed she was angry, I knew I'd get a spanking with a belt when the younger kids went outside, unless I hid upstairs and even that might not work. It wouldn't be because of anything I'd done. It was just because she was mad at her thoughts.

CHAPTER 8

When I asked Dad what was wrong with her, he would only say, "She's sick." I knew she wasn't sick like with a stomachache. So, I didn't quite understand until she had to go into the hospital and was on the psychiatric floor. Grandma told me it was because she had some emotional issues she had to work through.

All I knew was that she was where the people who were considered crazy or insane were. I never wanted to be insane if that was what was wrong with my mother. I was sad for her. However, it was a respite when she would go into the hospital, which usually coincided with summers when we were out of school. I guess three of us being at home was too much for her to take.

A MOTHER AT EIGHT

From the time I was eight and my little sister was born, I stood in for Mom. I felt like I was the mother. If Mom didn't fix supper, I would. If she didn't change my sister's diaper, I would. If she didn't wash the clothes, dry them, and put them away, I would. I felt it was my duty as the oldest sibling.

Dad and Grandma both praised me for helping out. It felt like the one thing I could do for my family.

When Mom was hospitalized and I was around 10 and older, I watched the kids. Dad would be there every day by five and leave every morning at seven. We made it through those times because I knew I could call on any of about four neighbors, one or two of whom were always at home and would check on us.

When Mom was sick, all I wanted was peace and calm. It was unsettling to not know how to respond to her. Although I didn't know these Bible verses at the time, they remind me today of how I felt when I didn't know what to do. "I'm slipping. I'm falling. Your love, God, took hold and held me fast. When I was upset and beside myself, You calmed me down and cheered me up" (Psalms 94:18-19 MSG).

I didn't know those exact words, but I would pray my own simple child-like prayer. "Jesus, Help me. Keep me calm even when Mom is mad." This was really hard for a kid and there were times she and I went toe-to-toe. What she yelled at me about wouldn't make sense.

I really think sometimes she saw me as someone else. Someone from her past that she was angry with. I never did figure out who that was, but at times she would call me someone else's name.

> Grandma wasn't the least bit crazy and she cooked delicious foods.

Contrast this with times I'd get to go to Grandma's house and spend the weekend or sometimes a month in the summer. There everything seemed perfect, completely idyllic. I'd help her with all her chores. We'd bake cookies and cakes and pies. At Grandma's there was no limit to what I could eat.

It made a whole lot of sense to me to equate food with sanity. Grandma was sane. She wasn't the least bit crazy. and she cooked delicious foods all the time. It became ingrained in me that Grandma's way of doing life was sane and my mother's way was insane.

The other thing about my mother is that she didn't want us to eat between meals. We only had canned fruit for dessert and there was usually just enough food for each of us. So, no overeating. Occasionally, she'd let me bake cookies, but it

CHAPTER 8

wasn't like Grandma's. The cookies were given out one at a time. We couldn't go get them whenever we wanted.

Now try for a moment to get inside my head as an eight-year-old. Mom is in the psychiatric ward at the hospital. I've been told she is emotionally ill or what others call crazy.

When she was at home, we couldn't have all the food we wanted and especially not all the sweets we wanted. She was angry at me a lot even though I did the things that needed to be done. I didn't even think she loved me. It felt a lot like she saw me as competition.

> It seemed clear that good food and plenty of it was what kept people sane, calm, and in control.

On the other hand, I had my wonderful Grandma who gave me all the food I wanted, especially sweets. She gave me big bear hugs and constantly told me how much she loved me and thanked me for helping her with whatever chore we were doing. She was the most sane and put together person I knew. I wanted to be just like her.

Her main job was cooking for her husband and helpers on the farm. I could eat all I wanted when I was there. All that helped me to put together my remedy for insanity.

If I looked at Mom versus Grandma, it seemed clear that good food and plenty of it was what kept people sane, calm and in control. I figured if I would cook like Grandma and eat what I wanted whenever I wanted, then I would be kind, loving, and beautifully peaceful like Grandma. It's what I desired.

How could I fight against inheriting my mother's insanity? One thing was clear to me. I needed the foods I loved and plenty of them. My main goal in life from the time I was a child was to not be like my mother in any way shape or form. I decided if I wanted a peaceful life, the way to get it was by eating Grandma's comfort foods.

EMOTIONAL MAKEUP

Our emotional make-up is formed when we are children. Our mothers or mother figures are the ones who are supposed to provide the basic needs of comfort and teaching. My mother was very discomforting and as far as I can remember, the only thing she taught me was the wonder of getting lost in a book. I do thank her for that.

The basic skills like cooking, washing dishes, folding clothes, and grocery shopping, I learned from Grandma. Anything I wanted to know, I just asked her. Grandma equaled stability, sanity, and food. Therefore, food equaled stability and sanity, especially the kinds of foods I learned to cook with Grandma's instructions. Food kept me sane.

I never wanted my emotions to be like my mother's which were happy one minute, sad the next, and angry any time I looked at her. I wanted my emotions to be on a level line. I didn't want to have any highs, lows, or angry outbursts. I wanted my emotions to be on a straight line with no feelings at all. I couldn't trust my emotions because I couldn't trust how Mom might act on any given day.

Being at Grandma's where there was an unending supply of great foods meant I could eat all I wanted. Food was my medicine, and it was much better than the drugs my mother took, which seemed to make her check out of life.

CHAPTER 8

The things we learn as children stay with us throughout our lives and guide our emotions until we figure out what we've really been doing to ourselves is anything but sane. The habits we learn along the way also stay with us until we understand how and why we must change them.

All my adult years up until 2004 were spent in super morbid obesity. There is no way I could elevate food to the status I did and not gain a tremendous amount of weight. Just because we become an adult and we know that eating all the food we want is ruining our health, the reasoning of our inner child is still there with us until we understand what we are doing and why.

It was like there was a little girl inside me directing my emotions, especially where food was concerned. There was the adult voice, but because the adult loved Grandma's food she agreed with the little girl who was driving my emotions. Of course, the evil one agreed with both. He really didn't have to work hard at tempting me. I was eagerly eating into the feeding frenzy.

STEPS TOWARDS TRANSFORMATION

Finally, there came the time when I understood that I was slowly killing myself eating the way Grandma had taught me and I started on my lifestyle transformation journey.

I was in a group with others who had life-controlling issues like food and alcohol. My mentor was a long-time sober alcoholic, so we were going through the 12 steps of Alcoholics Anonymous and applying those to our situations.

The first step I had no problem with. I admit I am powerless over food, mainly foods containing sugar and that my life has become unmanageable. I could just look at myself and see that was true. To validate that, I could look back over all the times I had lost weight only to gain it back when I started eating what I wanted. That moving picture in my mind was proof of how very unmanageable and distressing being super morbidly obese was. I could admit this very easily.

Calling my weight gain unmanageable and likening what I was doing to what an alcoholic does, helped me understand in order to manage food I had to stop eating sugar.

Thankfully, this is when my mentor introduced me to how to begin to change my habits. It's not a quick process. It's a step-by-step, slow, and steady process that we continue for the rest of our lives.

THE HARDEST STEP

Steps one and three I had no problem with. Step three states that I made a decision to turn my will and my life over to the care of God. This is the surrender step. I knew this was a moment-by-moment surrender for the rest of my life and I was fine with that.

I skipped over step two because for me it was the hardest of all of the steps. It simply says I came to believe that a power greater than myself can restore me to sanity. I couldn't go there. I couldn't admit that because if I did, I would be admitting that I was insane.

My life-long goal was to show the world that I was not insane like my mother. I didn't like it, but I knew what I had been doing was in fact insane.

This was the first time I realized that I was using food to attempt to normalize my emotions. Before this time, I would say I was not an emotional eater. It was finally very clear to me that this was a lie. The more I ate the more I could anesthetize any pain and, therefore, keep my emotions at non-disruptive level.

I would eat when I was sad, weepy, overwhelmed, stressed, frustrated, angry, upset, confused, embarrassed, unsure, disgusted, dejected, desperate, annoyed, or irritated. I would eat when I was enthusiastic, happy, or overjoyed because even the good feelings could get out of control like they did with my mother.

> God showed me I was using food to medicate my emotions and try to turn them off.

God showed me that I was using food to medicate my emotions and try to turn them off. Any food with too much sugar or carbohydrate content would anesthetize my emotions so I didn't have to feel them. It gave me a high that was euphoric but would wear off very quickly. Then I would want more sugary foods to get to the state that had become the place I wanted to stay. Sugar was my drug of choice. It was what made me feel what I described as normal.

It started out as something I saw as good that would help me through life, but it quickly took control of my life. I could easily call it unmanageable because at the time someone would just have to look at me weighing 430 pounds and see that was true.

To say I needed to be restored to sanity was difficult for me to admit. What finally helped me was to realize that it was insane to allow myself to gain the amount of weight I had. It's even more insane than what my mother went through because I did that to myself.

My mother had a chemical imbalance. In her later years with spiritual counseling, changing psychiatrists, cutting down on her meds, finding fun hobbies to take part in, visiting with friends she trusted, and hanging on to Jesus as tight as she could, she managed her life and was able to be a wonderful grandma to her grandchildren.

There was no chemical imbalance in me. I just loved the foods Grandma fed me, and I was rebelling against the way my mother saw food.

LIFE IS EMOTIONAL

I finally admitted I needed to be restored to sanity and it might even be OK to not be even keel all the time. Life is full of emotions. That's what makes life so great. It's OK to cry if I am sad or deeply moved. It's OK to laugh out loud. It's OK to put my arms around someone who needs a hug. It's OK to talk about my emotions and admit it when I am frustrated. It's OK to be honest with someone and tell them they are annoying if it's really bothering me. It's especially OK to love someone and tell them that.

The scriptures have a lot to say about emotions. "A calm and peaceful and tranquil heart is life and health to the body, but passion and envy are like rottenness to the bones" (Proverbs 14:30 AMP).

This is talking about negative emotions, such as jealousy, anger, frustration, unforgiveness, and even fear. These are the runaway emotions I didn't know how to manage, instead I tried to medicate them with food, so they'd go away. Emotions don't really go away, though. They just hide until the moment

CHAPTER 8

when some issue triggers them and they come back with greater vengeance.

What I really longed for was to be and feel healthy. This same verse in The Passion Translation tells us a tender and tranquil heart will make us healthy. The Message says a sound mind makes a healthy body.

Sound mind should sound familiar. Paul said, "God did not give us a spirit of timidity or cowardice or fear, but He has given us a spirit of power and of love and of sound judgment and personal discipline, abilities that result in a calm, well-balanced mind and self-control" (2 Timothy 1:7 AMP).

All my life I had been longing for peace. I felt that at Grandma's but not at home with Mom. There was always tension. David said in Psalms 27:3 MSG that when we are besieged, we can be as calm as a baby because God is there.

His son, Solomon, admonished, "Can you bridle your tongue when your heart is under pressure? That's how you show that you are wise. An understanding heart keeps you cool, calm, and collected, no matter what you're facing" (Proverbs 17:27 TPT).

MY SECRET WEAPON

I began to understand the Holy Spirit was and is my secret weapon. Overeating was just a distraction the enemy had provided and continued to encourage in my life. When we truly understand and have surrendered to the Holy Spirit's power, which is infinitely greater than ours, He can and will restore us to sanity. It's the answer I cling to today.

"God stilled the storm, calmed the waves and hushed the hurricane to only a whisper," (Psalm 107:29 TPT). He will do the same for me and you. David also proclaimed, "I will hurry off to hide in the higher place, into my shelter, safe from this raging storm and tempest" (Psalms 55:8 TPT).

We can pour out all our worries and stress on Him and leave them there because He always tenderly cares for us, as it says in I Peter 5:7 TPT.

David said there are times God wants us to have our passion for life restored, to really feel the pleasures He has for us. "Let my passion for life be restored, tasting joy in every breakthrough you bring to me. Hold me close to you with a willing spirit that obeys whatever you say" (Psalms 51:12 TPT).

> God admonishes us to reveal and not hide our emotions.

Worry is something that's hard to deal with, but Jesus said, "Refuse to worry about tomorrow, but deal with each challenge that comes your way, one day at a time. Tomorrow will take care of itself" (Matthew 6:34 TPT).

God also told us to reveal and not hide our emotions, "With tender humility and quiet patience, always demonstrate gentleness and generous love toward one another, especially toward those who may try your patience" (Ephesians 4:2 TPT). When we do this, we show the love of Jesus towards others.

Did you know there is something more glorious we can feast on than the best food we've ever eaten? "Feast on all the treasures of the heavenly realm and fill your thoughts with heavenly realities, and not with the distractions of the natural realm" (Colossians 3:2 TPT).

CHAPTER 8

What would happen if we'd just think about the treasures of God more than food?

I can finally say I am not insane, but I can also admit that I was insane when I was gaining weight faster than a bullet train.

I'm embracing the fact that I am an emotional child of the King. He gifted me with my emotions and I'm happy to share them in the ways they should be used in order to fulfill the destiny He has given me. I hope you feel the same way.

Food is not necessary to calm us or keep us sane. We just need to surrender to Jesus and let Him lead us.

Jesus was emotional. He wept. He laughed. He loved. He even got angry over the money changers in the temple. Yet, even though His accusers called Him crazy, He was without a doubt the most sane man who ever lived.

I definitely want to be like Him.

PRAY THIS PRAYER

"Dear Jesus, help me to surrender to You my anxiety, stress, and emotions I don't want to deal with.

"Help me to just get quiet and still enough to hear Your voice speaking to me and leading me in the way You want me to go.

"Help me to understand I don't need sugary foods and junk foods to keep me sane. I have You. You are all I need.

"In Jesus name, Amen."

ANSWER THESE QUESTIONS

1. Where did you learn your relationship with food?

2. Do you feel like eating whatever you want whenever you want keeps you sane?

3. How do your emotions play a part in when and what you eat? Be honest.

4. Circle all the emotions that cause you to overeat or eat things you know are outside your boundaries: sad, weepy, overwhelmed, stressed, frustrated, angry, upset, confused, embarrassed, unsure, disgusted, dejected, desperate, annoyed, irritated, enthusiastic, happy, overjoyed.

5. If you circled even one of these, you are an emotional eater. We aren't supposed to eat from emotions. We are supposed to eat when our stomachs aren't full when we are truly physically hungry. How does physical hunger differ from emotional hunger?

CHAPTER 8

6. Journal about this quote and how it relates to you. "The Holy Spirit is my secret weapon. Overeating is just a distraction the enemy encouraged in my life."

7. How can the Holy Spirit restore you to sanity?

FOOD KEEPS ME SANE

CHAPTER 8

"Refuse to worry about tomorrow, but deal with each challenge that comes your way, one day at a time. Tomorrow will take care of itself"

MATTHEW 6:34 TPT

CHAPTER 9

FOOD WILL PROTECT ME

Protection is one of our core needs when we come into this world as helpless babies. The member of our biological or adopted family whose role it is to protect us is our father or father figure. Many who have grown up with single mothers or an absentee father feel their mother is fulfilling that need. In reality, if this need is filled, it will be by a father figure. Otherwise, we learn how to self-protect, probably by watching how our mother does it because one of our mother's roles is to teach us.

One of the main ways we self-protect is by making ourselves physically larger. Those of us who have food issues will self-protect by overeating. Even though the adult part of us wants to lose weight, we can't figure out why we keep eating. Part of it is an emotional need for protection.

As one woman said, "If I lose weight, I will look too attractive. I've been hurt by males in the past. I need to protect myself by being larger, so men won't come on to me." Another who had lost a significant amount of weight in the past and

CHAPTER 9

allowed herself to get involved in sexual relationships that she was ashamed of, felt if she lost weight, she might do that again.

By far the majority of women I deal with who are self-protecting with food have a root issue that began in childhood. Many who were abused at very young ages feel like it was their fault, rather than the abuser's fault.

They will say things like, if I hadn't gone into his room. If I hadn't gone into the boy's fort. If I hadn't been wearing shorts. They take the blame and therefore they feel the responsibility is theirs and as a result they have to self-protect. Many of these women have told no one about what happened to them because they felt in some way it was their fault.

Overeating is hard to control in these situations because the emotional side of us is being driven by the scared little girl who was molested. It might not have been a rape, although it could have been. It might have been a game of touching. I find most of the times this was initiated by a child other than themselves.

IT WASN'T MY FAULT OR WAS IT?

When I was six years old, an older boy in our neighborhood, invited me to come play doctor in the boys' fort. He and my little brother hung out together a lot, but it was always no girls allowed in the fort. I was excited that I was being privileged to see the inside of the fort.

I had gotten one of those plastic doctor kits for Christmas so I thought he really meant I could be his nurse and we'd play like we were doctors fixing up something. I brought my doctor kit to the fort. He asked my little brother to stay at the door of the fort to let us know if any new patients were coming. I still had no idea what playing doctor meant to him.

Inside the fort I gave him the doctor kit so he could see what we needed from there. He just set it aside and laughed and said he wouldn't need that. He told me to lie down and close my eyes because he was the doctor, and he was going to examine me.

> He started feeling me in places I knew Mom had told me no boy, except my husband, should ever touch.

He pulled up my shirt and was feeling around on my stomach and saying does this hurt, does this hurt. When I'd say no, he would say, "OK, we need to exam a little more."

That's when he pulled my shorts and underwear down and started feeling me in places I knew my mother had told me no boy or man except my husband should ever see, much less touch. I was frozen in time.

Then, my little brother stuck his head in the fort and saw what was happening. He said, "Sissy, we have to go. Daddy is calling us for supper." The older boy fled while I rearranged my clothes and ran as fast as I could. I didn't want Dad to know I had been in the fort with the boys.

At the supper table Dad asked, "Where were you when I called you? You took a long time to get home." I know he was looking right at me, but I was staring at my plate.

"We were in the fort," my little brother said.

"What were you doing?" This time it was my mother asking the question.

CHAPTER 9

I had no idea what to say. "Adam pulled Sissy's pants down," my naïve little brother said.

It felt like all the air in our little five-room house was sucked out with that statement. My mother, who was always the disciplinary parent, didn't know what to say. She looked at Dad.

Dad said, "Teresa, finish your supper and go to your room. Stay there until we come to talk to you."

I was sure I'd get a spanking because I did feel like it was partly my fault. After all, I willingly went to the fort alone with Adam. When they came in, Dad told me I couldn't play with Adam anywhere but in our yard and only if there were others there too. I couldn't go to his yard or in the wooded area around his yard.

It felt like I got punished for what he did to me. My mother had another talk with me, essentially telling me that as a girl it was my responsibility to protect myself.

IT WASN'T MY FAULT, RIGHT?

Fast forward to when I was 11 and was molested by an older friend of the family at Grandma's house. Everyone was downstairs and I was still in bed upstairs. When he came in the room, I played dead and kept my eyes closed.

I wanted to yell, kick, and scream, but I couldn't. I felt paralyzed with fear just like when my Grandma and I came upon a copperhead snake down by the creek when we were picking greens. She told me to stand as still as possible so the snake wouldn't strike and then slowly back away.

All I could do was silently pray, "Help me, Jesus. Help me, Jesus." Just when I was sure he was going to perform the act my mother had warned me about, his wife called him to breakfast from the bottom of the stairs.

He left, but not before he leaned in close and said gruffly. "Open your eyes." I didn't obey. I held my breath until I heard laughter. I knew he had joined his wife and my grandparents at the breakfast table.

SELF-PROTECTION WAS MY ONLY OPTION

I had planned to stay another couple of weeks at Grandma's while they were there, but I made the decision to leave and go home with my parents when they came that day for lunch.

I couldn't tell anyone what happened because I was afraid they would think it was my fault. Dad was the one always telling me not to wear shorts and short sleeve tops. It was summer and I had worn both that day. Maybe that's why he did what he did?

I couldn't tell my mother. I was sure she would believe the man. After all, I was the one who willingly went into the boys' fort when I was six. Of course, she would think it was my fault. No, the only thing I could do was protect myself.

I decided I would not spend any more nights at Grandma's when that man was there. I would stay away from where he was if at all possible. I would self-protect. When I grew up ,I would make sure I was big enough and strong enough to dissuade any man who acted like a copperhead snake.

These two incidents were a big part of the reason it took a long time before I could ever lose weight and keep it off. It felt

CHAPTER 9

too risky. Even after I got married to a loving man, I still felt the need to protect myself. It really hit home to me after I had lost 100 pounds the first time. I had gone to weigh on my lunch break and saw that I had reached my goal. I was so elated!

I bounded into the office building and got on the elevator up to the sixth floor. There happened to be a department director on there at the same time. When the elevator door closed, he looked me up and down and said, "You're looking really good."

I don't remember what else he said, but I took whatever was said as him coming on to me. I was on the elevator with a copperhead snake! As soon as the elevator door opened, I ran to my office. That day I went down on my break and got a diet soda and several candy bars. It was time to start self-protecting again.

FORGIVENESS IS THE KEY

To get through this, I had to forgive the older man for molesting me when I was 11. Before I did that anytime I thought of him he was like a monster looming over me with a venomous snake head. When I forgave him, I saw him like a shriveled up little old man. I said out loud, "God, I've been afraid of that all my life?"

However, I still felt the need to self-protect. It was there even though I had forgiven the man. Any time a man would say something to me that even hinted of sexual implication, I felt fear grip me again. I would run to food to protect me. Eating more food, though, is a false protection. Being larger does not mean you will not be molested.

The fear was there because I hadn't gone to the root of the situation which was the time with Adam in the fort when I was six. That was the first time this kind of thing happened, and I felt I was the one to blame. So, I chose to forgive Adam for misleading me, tricking me, manipulating me, lying to me, using me, molesting me, and making me feel guilty for what he did.

By this time, I had learned the second step in this process. I renounced the lie that Jesus will mislead me, trick me, manipulate me, lie to me, use me, and make me feel guilty for something I didn't do.

Then I asked Him, "Jesus what is Your truth?" He said to me softly and gently as only He can do, "I love you. You are my bride. I want nothing more than for you to lay back against me and breathe and feel my heartbeat. My heart beats for you and all creation to be in close relationship with Me."

These times with Father God, Holy Spirit, and Jesus when we renounce the lies we are believing and ask God to tell us His truth are some of the most profound I've ever had.

NO MORE FEAR OF MAN

A few months after this, my husband and I were on a trip and three specific things happened, which in the past would have scared me and made me afraid of the men involved. All three times Roy was nearby but not right by me. All three times I saw the actions or words for what they were, simply jokes from jovial guys and laughed them off. All three times I immediately recognized God was showing me I had changed.

I no longer have to self-protect with food because food does not protect me. If anything, it slows me down in case I really am in a difficult situation and need to run away. I now totally rely on Father God to be my protector.

CHAPTER 9

I also began to understand Dad really did try to protect me. That's why I felt it was my fault. He gave me boundaries to stay within when I was six. He gave me boundaries when I was older such as not wearing shorts or short-sleeve shirts. These were his ways of protecting me. However, they also made me afraid to tell him what happened.

I forgave him for that. I renounced the lie that Father God doesn't know how to protect me and asked Him what His truth is. The Bible is full of His promises to protect us. I may not always see Him in the various situations, but He is there. God was there in Dad calling us for supper when I was six. He was there in the older man's wife calling him to breakfast when I was 11.

GOD IS OUR PROTECTOR

God reminded me that He "is the bedrock under my feet, the castle in which I live, my rescuing knight. My God—the high crag where I run for dear life, hiding behind the boulders, safe in the granite hideout; My mountaintop refuge, He saves me from ruthless men. I sing to God, the Praise-Lofty, and find myself safe and saved" (II Samuel 22:3-4 MSG).

Whenever we are afraid it's because the evil one has his grips on us in some way. For me, it was fear of certain kinds of men, men who were like poisonous snakes. God is greater than those types of men. "But the Lord is faithful, and He will strengthen you and protect you from the evil one" (II Thessalonians 3:3 NIV).

God is not asleep or far away. He's always watching over us and knows who our enemies are and what they are capable of, but He is greater. "Be strong and courageous. Do not be afraid or terrified because of them, for the Lord your God goes with you; He will never leave you nor forsake you" (Deuteronomy 31:6 NIV).

Sometimes we are afraid that God won't hear us or save us because we have made bad choices. I felt that way with these situations even though they occurred when I was still a child and could have been so much worse.

GOD IS NEAR

I've come to understand that "The Lord is near to the brokenhearted and saves those crushed in spirit" (Psalm 34:18 NASB). He doesn't run from us. He draws closer to us to rescue us.

It's in our most difficult times that God makes Himself known even more to us. He said, "When you pass through the waters, I will be with you; and when you pass through the river, they will not sweep over you. When you walk through the fire, you will not be burned; the flame will not set you ablaze" (Isaiah 43:2 NIV).

God doesn't promise us an easy time here on this earth. There will be difficulties, but He said. "Weeping may last for the night, but joy will come in the morning" (Psalms 30:5 NIV).

If we have God, we can have peace in any situation. "The Lord is near. Do not be anxious about anything, but in every situation, by prayer and petition, with thanksgiving, present your requests to God. And the peace of God, which transcends all understanding, will guard your hearts and your minds in Christ Jesus" (Philippians 4:5-7 NIV).

CHAPTER 9

I love this promise. "May God Himself, the God of peace, sanctify you through and through. May your whole spirit, soul and body be kept blameless at the coming of our Lord Jesus Christ. The one who calls you is faithful, and He will do it" (I Thessalonians 5:23-24 NIV).

This is both a prayer and a promise. The God of peace is protecting us for all eternity. He is keeping everything about us blameless. The biggest protection is summed up in these few words. The One who calls you is faithful, and He will do it! Our part is to just trust Him and not lose hope.

Paul shared this unfiltered truth. "We also glory in our sufferings because we know that suffering produces perseverance; perseverance, character; and character, hope. And hope does not put us to shame, because God's love has been poured out into our hearts through the Holy Spirit, who has been given to us" (Romans 5:3-5 NIV).

Whatever we are going through the final answer is hope because we have the power of the Holy Spirit available to us at all times. We should never be afraid. He is always with us.

Through His Word, God gives us just a small glimpse of God's power. "Breathtaking and awesome is Your power! Astounding and unbelievable is Your might and strength when it goes on display!" (Psalms 89:13 TPT). Why do we think we have to self-protect? We only need to call on God and He comes to our rescue!

GOD IS OUR RESCUER

All through the Psalms God tells us that He will rescue us. "He will rescue you from every hidden trap of the enemy, and He will protect you from false accusation" (Psalms 91:3 TPT).

"Honor Me by trusting Me in your day of trouble. Cry aloud to Me, and I will be there to rescue you" (Psalms 50:15 TPT).

"God will be your bodyguard to protect you when trouble is near. Not one bone will be broken" (Psalms 34:20 TPT).

"Then we cried out, 'Lord, help us! Rescue us!' And He did!" (Psalms 107: 6, 13, 19 TPT).

I WILL RESCUE YOU

It reminds me of the Lauren Daigle song, "Rescue." I love the words of this song because I always feel like it is God singing this to me. He's singing it to you as well.

"You are not hidden. There's never been a moment You were forgotten. You are not hopeless, though you have been broken, your innocence stolen.

"I hear you whisper underneath your breath. I hear your SOS, your SOS. I will send out an army to find you in the middle of the darkest night. It's true, I will rescue you."

"I will never stop marching to reach you. In the middle of the hardest fight. It's true, I will rescue you. Oh, I will rescue you."[1]

Here's a few things I am absolutely confident about. The first is this "For the eyes of the Lord range throughout the earth to strengthen those whose hearts are fully committed to Him" (II Chronicles 16:9 NIV). If we are committed to Him, He's already got us taken care of.

Second, I, like Paul, am "confident of this, that He who began a good work in you will carry it on to completion until the day of Christ Jesus" (Philippians 1:6 NIV). Our destiny, our mission is secure in Him.

CHAPTER 9

And third, I am confident that when I cry out, my God is there, and He will rescue me.

PRAY THIS PRAYER

"Father God, thank You for caring enough to take care of me, protect me, and rescue me even when I may not feel like I deserve to be rescued.

"Help me forgive myself for the things that others have done to me that I have taken on as my own. Help me forgive others for the things they have done to me.

"Especially help me reconnect to You, by renouncing the lies I am believing about You.

"I need You so very much. Rescue me my Savior, my God.

"In Jesus name. Amen."

ANSWER THESE QUESTIONS

1. Do you think that food or being larger protects you? Why and in what way?

2. Have you had an encounter or encounters similar to what was described in this chapter. How do you feel about that incident today? Does it still affect you in any way? How does it affect you?

3. If you have had a similar situation, have you chosen to forgive the person?

4. If it was an older man or father figure, have you renounced the lie that Father God will mistreat you or not protect you? If not, do that now and ask Him what His truth is.

5. If it was a person your age, have you renounced the lie that Jesus will manipulate or use you? If not, do that now and ask Him what His truth is.

6. Are you trying to self-protect with food? Where has that gotten you?

7. Choose at least one verse about God's protection. Write it out on cards and put it where you can see it and refer to it often. If possible, memorize it so it's always with you.

CHAPTER 9

ENDNOTES

1. Daigle, Lauren. Lyrics to "Rescue." https://www.lyricsondemand.com/laurendaiglelyrics/rescuelyrics.html.

CHAPTER 10

FOOD IS MY FRIEND

Food is my friend. We all know that is a lie and an excuse we use for continuing to eat what we want. For years I counted on desserts made with sugar and flour like I would a best friend. I was like the woman who told me straight up, "Food is my friend." To her the kinds of foods she loved to eat were convenient and seemed to fill a void.

To me the desserts and high carb-laden foods were exactly like a person I could count on. They were always there. I thought this inanimate friend would always understand me and ease my stress, anxiety, overwhelm, frustration, anger, worry, sadness, pain, or any emotion I didn't want to feel. The foods I loved were always available because I was the one that made sure of that.

I felt like I controlled what I ate because I bought the things I loved and things that my Grandma had shown me how to cook. I bought them, fixed them, baked them, and ate them. Oh, my family helped with the eating, but without a doubt I was the one who consumed the most. That was evidenced by the amount of weight I had on my body. Even though the weight gain was the fault of my poor food choices, I still saw those foods as my friends because they were always there snuggling up close to me and whispering sweet nothings in my ear. "Bake another batch. You know you want more. Why deprive yourself? You deserve it."

TOO MUCH TO DO

I am an all or nothing person. I don't do anything halfway. That led me to fill my days to overflowing with meetings, volunteer work, family, and actual work to make money. This level of activity stressed me to the point that I felt I deserved all the treats I indulged in.

When I ate those things, I felt they calmed me and gave me what I wanted which was hundreds of small amounts of reprieve in the midst of stressful days and nights.

I had too much to do. I planned it that way intentionally because having nothing to do meant I had time to think, and I didn't want to think about what I was doing to my body. That might mean I'd have to say good-bye to foods made with sugar. I felt I couldn't live without them.

Sugar was not my friend. It was actually evil in disguise. It didn't care about me. It was a real tool of the devil, just like drugs or alcohol. It gave me a feeling of peace for a moment and then when the high wore off I had to have more to get the same feeling. I was like an alcoholic, only with sugar.

My mindset was crazy and so is yours if you think any type of food is your friend. We aren't supposed to have a relationship with sugar or any food. It's not a person and we should never treat it like that. Yet, some of us consider certain foods as our best friends.

When the truth hit me that I was treating sugar like a friend, I was raving mad at the devil and at sugar. Sugar snuck into my life and took over, slowly, slyly, cunningly, manipulating me with my demise in mind.

I had been captured by what I feel is one of the devil's most well-kept secret weapons. Once we discover that, it should be easier to tell it, "Good-bye." Then, we can finally say, "Hello" to the One who should be our best friend for all of eternity. This is my farewell address to sugar.

GOOD-BYE SUGAR

I thought we were good together and then you do this to me. You seemed to be there every time I needed you. I thought you made my life better and that we were the perfect team.

You listened when I cried and just your tangible presence comforted me in a way I thought none other could. You made me feel better even if only for a few minutes and that's all I cared about at the time.

You were my companion in the good times and the bad. If I was lonely, you were right there with me. It didn't matter that I didn't know who to call because you were there. You soothed the pain of loneliness.

When I was tired, you were the one that gave me a pick me up. You made me feel like I had energy to go on even if for just a few more minutes. It felt like life was better with you.

When I was ready to blow my top, you were there soothing me. Just one whiff of you and I knew all my problems were gone. You calmed me and made the anger go away. If it came back, you were there to help me again. You always did your job.

When stress would overwhelm me, I would run straight to you. You were the best at making me forget about everything I had to do and just focus on my needs and wants in the moment. You seemed to take care of them all.

PROTECTOR

You protected me to make sure no men would get close and take advantage of me. I knew with you by my side I was always safe because you filled the distance between me and danger.

I never had to field off those who wanted to take advantage of me. You gave me a cushion against the world. You made them all go away and leave me alone.

You cozied up to me so that you were all I wanted. I felt if I had you, I didn't need anything else.

Even in good times, you made everything better. Just one look at you and I knew I would soon be satisfied, even if it was only for a short time. You made everything worth it.

You helped me celebrate when I had worked long hours, and no one noticed or when I met a self-imposed deadline and wanted to reward myself. You were always my first choice.

DECEIVER

Now, I learn with all we've been through you have not had my best interests at heart. You have been deceiving me. As a matter of fact, you had the path planned for my demise, destruction, and eventual death. And to think that I trusted you with my very life.

Why would you do that to me? What did I ever do to you? You were my everything. My comforter, companion, protector, lover, and friend.

I heard the doctor. I know you've been trying to kill me. And for once I look at you and do not want you in my life anymore.

Because, for once, I'm choosing life, my life, my destiny, my purpose. I'm deciding that I'm worth more than a cookie or a piece of my favorite cake. I'm worth more than the best ice cream I can buy and the most decadent brownie ever made.

KILLER

So this is it. We've had a long journey together and it's been downhill all the way. You no longer are in control of me.

All my life, you've been slowly destroying me and I have been letting you.

You are not a comfort at all. You make me extremely uncomfortable. You are no friend. You seek to harm me.

You do not help me have energy. You spike my energy for a minute and then I crash and burn.

You do not give me peace when I am angry. You only help me stuff my anger, so it impacts every part of my life.

You do not relieve my stress. You add pounds to my body which increases my stress and taxes my heart.

You do not protect me. You are the one thing that is systematically destroying me leaving me vulnerable to every disease imaginable.

CHAPTER 10

GOOD-BYE FOREVER

This is good-bye forever. You are no longer my friend. I see you for the monster you are.

Sugar, you are out of my life for good. Oh, and don't try coming back. I will not change my mind.

I know now, I have been putting you above God in my life, above my own desire to live. I will no longer do that. God is my comforter, companion, and protector. No substance can provide for me like He can. I see you for what you are. You are a tool of the devil in my life.

I am finally free of you and believe me, nothing tastes as good as freedom feels. Nothing!

WHO IS MY FRIEND?

I've shared this story many times through the years because I really believe the devil used sugar to try to destroy me. He will use whatever your favorite food is to destroy you, as well.

You may wonder if sugar or other foods aren't your friends, then who is? We all have friends, but they aren't like our favorite go-to food that is always available to munch on. What, if anything, is meant to be our friend?

Solomon said, "There is a friend who sticks closer than a brother." (Proverbs 18:24 NIV). That friend is Jesus.

I know. It's hard to understand that because we can't see Jesus, Father God, or the Holy Spirit. So how do we know He is there? Like any best friend, we have to develop a personal relationship with Him. It's not about attending church or knowing all the right scriptures. It's about talking with God like you'd talk with your best friend.

MY BEST FRIEND

When I think about the person who is my best friend, I have to say it is my husband. I realized that he is the friend I have that is the most like Jesus. He would do anything for me that he could do because he not only loves me, but he is my friend.

As great as my husband is, though, I know that God wants me to understand He is my very best friend who sticks closer than a brother. This verse is not talking about our spouses, though, because as close as I am to my husband, one day we may be separated. We have a pact that we will go to heaven at the same time, but we all know that rarely happens.

Jesus is the member of the Godhead who is closest to us because He knows what it is like to be human. Paul tells us that Jesus became a human willingly. He did it out of love for us so that He could live a sinless life, become the supreme sacrifice for our failures, and so that we would have a clear path to salvation. That's love that denotes a friend who is closer than any human being alive today.

It's hard to wrap our brains around how Jesus, who is part of the Trinity, was fully man when He was here on earth.

Paul said in Philippians 2:5-11 TPT, "Consider the example that Jesus, the Anointed One, has set before us. Let His mindset become your motivation. He existed in the form of God, yet He gave no thought to seizing equality with God as His supreme prize.

CHAPTER 10

"Instead, He emptied Himself of His outward glory by reducing Himself to the form of a lowly servant. He became human. He humbled Himself and became vulnerable, choosing to be revealed as a man and was obedient. He was a perfect example, even in His death—a criminal's death by crucifixion!

"Because of that obedience, God exalted Him and multiplied His greatness! He has now been given the greatest of all names! The authority of the name of Jesus causes every knee to bow in reverence! Everything and everyone will one day submit to this name—in the heavenly realm, in the earthly realm, and in the demonic realm. And every tongue will proclaim in every language: 'Jesus Christ is Lord,' bringing glory and honor to God, His Father!"

NO GREATER LOVE

Jesus chose to become a human and die on a cross for us. There is no greater kind of friend than this. He is the friend who is always there and sticks closer than any person we have ever known, loved, or trusted. He is the epitome of a best friend.

Not only did Jesus become human to die a sinless death on the cross, He is our high priest. "Therefore, since we have a great high priest who has passed through the heavens, Jesus the Son of God, let's hold firmly to our confession.

"For we do not have a high priest who cannot sympathize with our weaknesses, but One who has been tempted in all things just as we are, yet without sin.

"Therefore, let's approach the throne of grace with confidence, so that we may receive mercy and find grace for help at the time of our need" (Hebrews 4:14-16 NASB).

THREE VITAL THINGS

Three things from this passage are vital to our lives as Christians.

1. We have an obligation to hold tight to Jesus because He is a friend who loves us and died for us.

2. As a human He was perfect and sinless. He had the same fleshly temptations we have but did not indulge. That means He will help us resist, as well.

3. Jesus is always there listening to us and prescribing mercy and grace to help us with any need we have.

WHAT ARE YOU DOING?

Our best friend, Jesus, also willingly helps us when we are tempted and find ourselves ready to indulge when we know we shouldn't. "The temptations in your life are no different from what others experience. And God is faithful. He will not allow the temptation to be more than you can stand. When you are tempted, He will show you a way out so that you can endure" (I Corinthians 10:13 NLT).

When I started my transformation journey and started to eat something I knew I shouldn't, Jesus, my best friend, was there simply asking me a question. "What are you doing?" I'd say, "I'm throwing this food away or I'm driving away from this fast-food place."

He wanted me to think about my commitment and what eating that might do to me because He did not, and still does not, want me to go back into bondage to the evil one.

CHAPTER 10

There is another verse that takes on a different meaning when we are talking about friendship with God. "You were God's expensive purchase, paid for with tears of blood, so by all means, then, use your body to bring glory to God!" (1 Corinthians 6:20 TPT).

God paid a high price for us. It was paid for with the blood of His only Son. Father God cried that day. The world went dark when life went out of His Son hanging on the cross. God, who wants us to be His friend, tells us that we can show Him that we are His friends by simply using our bodies to bring glory to Him.

AM I JESUS' FRIEND?

Jesus called His disciples His friends, but it had criteria attached to it. "You are my friends if you keep on doing what I command you. I do not call you servants any longer, for the servant does not know what his master is doing; but I have called you My friends, because I have revealed to you everything that I have heard from My Father" (John 15:14-15 AMP).

How do we show Jesus that we are His friends? By doing what He tells us to do. When we ask Jesus what to do about anything we are about to do here on earth and He shows us what we should do, if we do that then we are His friends.

Sometimes, though, we hear what Jesus wants us to do and we agree to it, but then we get busy doing what we want, and we don't realize our own life could be on the line if we don't listen and follow through. God has our good in mind, not our disaster, as Jeremiah 29:11 NLT says.

Many times in the past I didn't do what God told me to do because I didn't understand the why behind it. When God told me to stop eating sugar that first time, it was in order to save my life. I didn't do what He said until I got a death sentence proclaimed over me by a doctor. God was talking to me the entire time, but I excused it away.

God was asking me to do something because He trusted me. When I didn't do what He said, I really was not His friend, yet. It took me 30 more years to actually do what He told me to do. I am so glad I did. I am so glad I exchanged my friendship with sugar for friendship with God.

God has already demonstrated He is our friend. Evangelist D. L. Moody had a simple rule. It was "to treat the Lord Jesus Christ as a personal friend. His is not a creed, a mere doctrine, but it is He Himself we have."

I know that Jesus is my friend because He keeps leading me. A friend wouldn't keep on helping me if I was always going the other way. It doesn't matter what I do, God still wants to know about my day and whether it was awesome or horrific, whether I stayed within my food boundaries or pigged out. He's there to listen and guide. I have no other friend who does that like He does.

Only Author Max Lucado could come up with these words. "If God had a refrigerator, your picture would be on it. If He had a wallet, your photo would be in it. He sends you flowers every spring and a sunrise every morning. Face it, Friend. He is crazy about you!"

JESUS WANTS TO KEEP US SAFE

One of the reasons Jesus wants to be our friend is to keep us safe and free from the evil one. If we follow Him we will be. "We have freedom, for Christ has set us free! We must always

CHAPTER 10

cherish this truth and stubbornly refuse to go back into the bondage of our past" (Galatians 5:1 TPT).

The bondage of my past was foods made with sugar and flour. What was yours?

Understanding what held us in bondage is a big key towards not returning to it. All we have to do is listen to God when we are once again indulging in what we know He doesn't want us to.

When God asks, "What are you doing?" that means it's time to stop and evaluate what we should be doing instead.

PRAY THIS PRAYER

"Lord Jesus, I want to be Your friend. I want to follow what You tell me to do. I don't want food or other substances to be what I rely on. I want to rely only on You.

"You are the One who feeds me. You are the One who cares about me. You are my Companion, Protector and Comforter. Help me to see only You as the friend who is always there and who always has my best interests at heart.

"In your name I pray, Amen."

ANSWER THESE QUESTIONS

1. What are some reasons why you think or have thought food was your friend? What did you think it was doing for you?

2. In what ways have the foods you love not been a friend to you?

3. How has overeating the kind of foods you love been slowly killing you?

4. Why do you think you allowed yourself to become enslaved by these foods?

5. Who is your best friend on earth and why?

6. What do you have to do to make sure Jesus is your best friend? See John 15:14-15 AMP.

CHAPTER 10

7. Read Galatiand 5:1 TPT. What was the bondage of your past? Are you willing to stubbornly refuse to go back into that bondage? How will you guard against that?

FOOD IS MY FRIEND

CHAPTER 10

"At last we have freedom, for Christ has set us free! We must always cherish this truth and stubbornly refuse to go back into the bondage of our past."

GALATIANS 5:1 TPT

CHAPTER 11

DON'T ROCK THE LOVE BOAT

There's an excuse that comes up primarily when I'm talking one on one with a wife of a caring husband. She is so concerned about offending her husband that she can't tell him she no longer wants him to bring her candy as a gift. She wants to lose weight and knows candy is part of the reason she is overweight, but she is afraid of hurting his feelings. She's afraid of rocking the love boat they have created.

These are hard-working husbands who come home at the end of the day with a treat for their wives. It's something the husband has been doing for a long time and something the wife has always enjoyed. It filled her love tank to know her husband made a special stop just for her.

He had no idea candy was literally her downfall. He had no idea he was helping her gain weight and become unhealthy. She had programmed him to make that happen.

If this is you, let me just say your husband is not the one to blame. You are. You taught him what you wanted, and he is just following through. Every time he brought candy as a gift

CHAPTER 11

to you and your eyes lit up; it reinforced his effort to please you.

Here's the core question. Are you just making an excuse so you can continue to eat the candy your man brings you or do you really want to stop indulging in what you know is adding extra pounds to your body?

DO YOU REALLY WANT TO EAT HEALTHY?

If you really want to begin to eat healthy and you feel this is a major issue for your marriage, you must talk to him. Have a heart-to-heart conversation. Let him know you are beginning a healthy living journey and you need his help. Explain to him what you will be eating and that it would really help you if he would not bring candy, cookies, donuts, ice cream, and any sweets home to you.

Let him know that you love candy, but you are committed to not eating it anymore. Ask him to help you by not bringing that home to you as a gift. Give him some suggestions that would be better for you, such as flowers or a card.

Be honest with yourself before you have this conversation. Many back off from doing this because they don't want their husbands to know what they are doing in case they can't follow through with their plans. However, if you are really wanting to begin a healthy eating journey, it is imperative that you have those closest to you understand you are like an alcoholic only with sugar. You are a sugar addict, and it is off limits for you.

If you really are wanting to cut sugar out, you have to settle it within yourself that you are committed to learning how to give up sugar. This may not mean stopping it all at once but taking a habit change approach, which I teach in my Overcomers Christian Weight Loss Academy.

When pondering this, you may think nothing would give you more pleasure than eating something sweet. I totally get where you are because I've definitely been there. However, I'm not there now and I'm so grateful. I've learned sugar is not the ultimate pleasure. It's not even close. However, we have elevated it to that status in our lives and our husbands know how important is has been to us. Now, though, it's become a reminder of what we shouldn't do.

GOD WANTS US HEALTHY, NOT DEPRIVED

The aging Apostle John knew that God wants us healthy, not deprived. He said, "Beloved, I wish above all things that you may prosper and be in health, even as your soul prospers" (3 John 1:3 NKJV). Being prosperous really means being healthy in all ways—physically, mentally, emotionally, and spiritually.

If our bodies aren't healthy, we can't fulfill the destiny God has for us. Even though we know we should be more vigilant about the health of our bodies, we have a huge disconnect about following through when everyone around us is eating dessert. It begins to feel like it's us against the world.

Jesus talked about this when He prayed to the Father for us. "I'm not asking You to take them out of the world, but to keep them safe from the evil one. They do not belong to this world any more than I do" (John 17:15-16 NLT).

He understood that being in the world and not of the world is difficult. How can we be in the world but not succumb to earthly pleasures that lead us down a treacherous path to an early death by candy, cookies, donuts, and ice cream?

CHAPTER 11

Here's a scenario to consider. You've decided to give up sugar. It just so happens that your husband's family is having a big reunion and you know they are the world's best cooks. You've gained 20 pounds just thinking about all the desserts and other great foods that will be there. How do you guard yourself against indulging without hurting their feelings and your husband's feelings?

STEP 1—HAVE A CONVERSATION AND A PLAN

If you are going to be successful, you first have to get your husband on your side. Ask him to be like your guardian angel so you don't overindulge. Maybe even have a secret code, such as, "You're beautiful," which he whispers in your ear when he sees that it's difficult for you to say, "No." It also reinforces that he is helping you in a nice way. Praise him when he does. Let him know you appreciate his efforts.

Focus on what is important in the moment—your husband and the family members. Focus on talking with everyone, greeting people, and interacting. Try to find out one new thing you didn't know before about every person present. Laugh about old times. Enjoy the company.

STEP 2—BRING HEALTHY FOOD YOU CAN EAT

At any family or church gathering, be sure to bring healthy foods you can eat. Some suggestions are a fresh fruit salad, lettuce salad, grilled chicken, or some other kind of meat that is not breaded or fried. These types of foods go quickly so set aside a small portion for yourself.

One of my secret weapons is the only protein bar I've found that is low sugar. They are called Marigold Primal bars[1] and have 1.5 grams of sugar from raw maple syrup, 22 grams of protein, 3 carbs and are gluten-free and GMO-free. They are not sweet, but they make me think I have had a treat. I stick one in my purse to know I have it if I need it. Planning ahead really helps me stay on track.

STEP 3—CHANGE YOUR MINDSET

We change our minds about everything all the time. We might have changed what we are going to wear three times this morning. In order to change our mindsets to do the right thing we need to focus on God and let Him change us.

Paul said, "Don't become so well-adjusted to your culture that you fit into it without even thinking. Instead, fix your attention on God. You'll be changed from the inside out. Readily recognize what He wants from you, and quickly respond to it. Unlike the culture around you, always dragging you down to its level of immaturity. God brings the best out of you, develops well-formed maturity in you" (Romans 12:1-2 MSG).

We must fix our attention on God and only then will we be changed on the outside. Change has to begin inside us, in our minds. We have to set our minds to do what we know God wants us to do in order to change. We can't continue doing what we've always done and lose weight. It doesn't work that way.

We change by realizing the culture around us, and even the people we love, may not be addicted to sugar, but we are. Therefore, God tells us that we must do what we know is best for us.

CHAPTER 11

STEP 4—CONSTANT RENEWAL

One major mindset shift for me was that I do not need sugar to live. I won't die if I don't eat it, but I might have if I continued to eat things made with processed sugar. The key here is not to just change your mind once, but to allow your mind to be constantly renewed.

"Be constantly renewed in the spirit of your mind having a fresh mental and spiritual attitude. And put on the new nature, the regenerate self, created in God's image, Godlike in true righteousness and holiness" (Ephesians 4:22-23 AMP).

> Our old ways of thinking of ourselves as big, fat losers must change.

If we have accepted Christ, we must have a fresh mental and spiritual attitude about ourselves. "This means that anyone who belongs to Christ has become a new person. The old life is gone; a new life has begun!" (II Corinthians 5:17 NLT).

Our old ways of thinking about ourselves as big, fat losers must change. The old is gone. A new life has begun. If I think of myself in negative terms, I will act that way. Instead, I must begin to think of myself as a dearly beloved daughter of the King, ransomed, redeemed, sanctified, made holy and righteous, seated in heavenly places with Christ Jesus, with a destiny greater than anything I can think, dream, ask, or imagine!

"Never doubt God's mighty power to work in you and accomplish all this. He will achieve infinitely more than your greatest request, your most unbelievable dream, and exceed your wildest imagination! He will outdo them all, for His miraculous power constantly energizes you" (Ephesians 3:20 MSG).

Reading and re-reading that verse changed my mindset from I can't do this to I can do all things if and only if I allow Christ to give me strength as Philippians 4:13 tells us. Jesus Christ is the one who gives me the power to surrender the things I crave and to live this Christian life. I need His strength to do that every single day.

STEP 5—PLEASURE WITHOUT SUGAR

Kathleen DesMaisons gives great advice to sugar addicts in her book, *Potatoes Not Prozac*. She advocates consistent eating times, good protein, good fats, good breakfasts, and slowly getting rid of sugar as part of the ways to combat our craving for sweets.

This is because if you are a sugar addict, you are metabolically broken. You have unstable blood sugar and low beta endorphins and serotonin levels. Eating something sweet may seem like the quickest and easiest way to feel better, but it is also the quickest and easiest way to gain weight.

Sugar triggers the reward center in our brains. When we eat it, our brains constantly cry out for more and more. When we give it more sugar, it gives us a momentary high which quickly fades. Then we need more to get that same feeling again. This is a result of unstable blood sugar levels in our bodies.

There are other healthier activities that release beta endorphins into our bodies and raise our serotonin levels making us feel better. Here are some examples adapted from DesMaisons' list, with my added focus on the spiritual dimension, as well as other things we can do. I'm going to just start out with my favorite first so you'll know what that is and will remember it.

1. Orgasm with your loving and committed spouse
2. Consistent exercise of all types
3. Healthy meditation on the Word of God
4. Balance between moving and being still
5. Listening to Christian music
6. Prayer, both silent and vocal
7. Listening to Christian podcasts
8. Eating the right kind of food prepared the right way
9. Cooking and baking healthy foods
10. Dancing or doing other aerobic activities
11. Working in your garden or being outside
12. Listening to inspirational talks and spiritual messages
13. Enjoying a hobby you can get lost in
14. Reading a good book, preferably Christian
15. Gardening
16. Arranging flowers
17. Being with people, puppies, kitties that you love
18. Journaling
19. Writing poetry, short stories, and books
20. Painting, drawing or any kind of arts and crafts

The first time I read this list, I realized I dearly loved all of these things and yet, for years I had been choosing sugary treats over them. For me the biggest change was noticeable with consistent exercise. I love to exercise in the water. Even now, it has to be something really important for me to miss my exercise time. My time in the water calms me, energizes me, and gives me focus and clarity. It refreshes me and brings me alive spiritually, physically, and emotionally.

I could talk about each item on the list because they are all pleasures I have ramped up in my life. Every one of them, especially the first one, are much better than sugar. Talk about not rocking the love boat, your husband should enjoy number one, as well.

STEP 6—CHOOSE

We probably have certain foods we eat when we feel certain emotions. Write down some emotions that make you want to eat. Then write down what you are inclined to eat when you feel that emotion. Next, list some other things from the list of healthy pleasures you could do instead of eating.

My list includes journaling, painting, reading, prayer, Bible study, and writing short stories, taking drives in the country, even decluttering. When I feel overwhelmed, I find decluttering a space I'm in often, such as my office, closets, dresser drawers, or bathroom storage cabinet is a great stress reliever. Stressed used to mean I'd fix a huge meal or a dessert and eat it. Now it means it is time to declutter.

When I am frustrated, I find journaling to be an active release. I get all the bottledup thoughts in my head out on paper. When I read it the next day, I can evaluate my thoughts much better.

The list you make will be a valuable resource when you are tempted to eat something you really shouldn't eat. It is also a

CHAPTER 11

way to begin new habits. Doing these things will make you feel much better than eating too much ever will.

I remember when my husband brought me a box of candy for Valentine's Day, and I hadn't had the conversation with him yet about not eating candy.

> Our husbands need direction in how to please us.

So, I told him how much I loved that he was thinking about me, but I have learned sugar is very addictive to me. If I eat one piece, I will want it all and that will start me sliding down a very slippery slope. I asked him to take the candy and put it somewhere I wouldn't find it.

He sat there for a minute and said, "What can I get you then?" Our husbands need direction in how to please us.

I said, "Get me a card, one that you picked out and that says what you want to say to me. If it's a special occasion, get me some jewelry like a necklace, ring, or bracelet. It doesn't have to be expensive. It will just be meaningful if it is from you."

These days he still buys me cards and jewelry, but he also does things every day, like bring me my cold bottle of water and Marigold bar in the morning for breakfast. He makes sure I have what helps me get started for the day. I do have the world's best husband.

I hope this has given you some things to think about. The most important thing is to let those around you know what your own eating boundaries are and stay within them yourself. Choose some things to do instead of eating. Eating is not meant to be the only thing we do for fun.

There's always good old number one on the list. It's my favorite and likely it's also your husband's, as well.

PRAY THIS PRAYER

"Dear Jesus, I love my husband. Help me to help him help me on my healthy living journey.

"Help him to understand I am eating healthy because I want to be around longer and love him more.

"Help me to be strong and follow the boundaries You have given me on my healthy living journey.

"In Your Name I pray. Amen."

ANSWER THESE QUESTIONS

1. How have you programmed your husband to bring unhealthy foods like candy to you as a gift? What will you suggest he do instead?

2. Is thinking your husband will be offended if you tell him not to bring you candy just an excuse for you to continue to eat it or do you really want to begin eating healthier? How bad do you want to stop eating sugar?

3. Why is it important to have your husband and others help you stay true to your healthy boundaries?

CHAPTER 11

4. What kind of healthy food could you bring to a carry-in dinner that you and others would love?

5. How can you constantly be renewing your mind to follow what God wants you to do?

6. What pleasures will you indulge in instead of eating sugar-laded foods?

7. How will these pleasures help you stay away from eating the foods you know are bad for you?

ENDNOTES

1. Marigoldbars.com. Here's my link: https://www.marigoldbars.com/?ref=12. (My favorite is the primal bars, ChocoChunky Pecan.)

CHAPTER 11

*"Never doubt God's mighty
power to work in you and
accomplish all this.
He will achieve infinitely more
than your greatest request,
your most unbelievable
dream, and exceed your
wildest imagination!
He will outdo them all,
for His miraculous power
constantly energizes you."*

EPHESIANS 3:20 MSG

CHAPTER 12

STOP ALL THE NOISE

Voices, voices everywhere. We hear them from friends, family and extended family, best friends, worst enemies, television, social media, music, podcasts, speakers, preachers, teachers, mentors, casual acquaintances, and total strangers in the line at the grocery store.

It makes us think we are going crazy. Our thoughts and decisions are somewhere in the mix. It becomes so overwhelming we can't focus on what they are saying. The noise is so loud it overtakes us, and we can't think. So, we just listen to and follow whatever voice is hollering at us the loudest. We want to just yell, "Stop all the noise!"

Our excuse for not doing what we know God wants us to do is there is too much noise in our heads. Our thoughts seem to compete and fight with each other. We have no way to figure out what we really are thinking because there are just too many thoughts to choose from.

One woman told me that the door of fear of losing weight was open in her life and that her mind was holding it open. It was different because usually the door of fear is open because of something a family member, or another person did or said to us when we were children.

For her, though, it was the myriad of influences in her thoughts that was making her feel paralyzed and afraid to move forward. The evil one was definitely fueling the constant chatter in her head surrounding food. He was feeding her excuses as to why she couldn't and never would be able to lose weight.

VOICE OF EVIL

Orchestrating all the noise is the voice of the evil one and his minions. He uses all the voices he can to con us into doing things that are not good for us. However, he can't read our minds or speak to us in our minds. He's not inside our heads.

He's more like a little evil imp sitting on our shoulder whispering in our ears. He is a fallen angel and angels can't read our minds, so the devil and his demons can't either. If the devil could read Job's mind he would have known that he shouldn't waste his time trying him because Job was solidly devoted to God.

The devil is a master at reading our actions. He can see, for instance, that we are frustrated, exhausted, overwhelmed, and emotionally spent just by our actions.

He can hear what we say. He can see what we do. He can tempt us with our favorite go-to food or some other thing, like alcohol, drugs, pornography, or overspending to help us anesthetize our emotions.

We have already preprogrammed these into our lives. They are called habits. The devil knows every single habit we have. He keeps track of what we do, how we do it, and the instigators that cause us to do those things.

PHD IN OUR WEAKNESSES

The devil has a PhD in our weaknesses. He knows what kinds of foods we go to when we are feeling any emotion and what we crave. We even begin to feel like his voice is our voice, but it's really just a spirit that can speak to us.

I don't know how it works because when he speaks to us only we can hear him. It's tailored just for us. From personal experience, I know his voice is entirely different from God's voice. It mixes with all the other voices we are allowing in through our ear-gates so it's difficult to distinguish.

The evil one hears and sees the same things we do, takes note of it, and mixes that in with what he thinks will motivate us to go against what God says is best. He has eons of experience in doing the same for the estimated 105 billion people who have been alive since time began.

He's doing this because he wants to destroy us and render our destinies ineffective. To bring it into modern terms, the devil has the equivalent of the greatest fireproof computer ever built down in hell. There he keeps track of every human and their responses to all kinds of difficulties.

If he is trying to get at you, he might send a demonic spirit to convince you that you are nothing, will never amount to anything, can't lose weight, will always give up, and are a failure. He'll tell you, "No, you shouldn't have eaten that, but here have some more." He will try to make you afraid to even try to lose weight, give up alcohol, get free of drugs, stop watching pornography, stop gambling, stop spending money you don't have, and on and on.

His goal is to put as much noise in your mind as he can so you listen only to your fleshly desires, which will lead to death. "For the sense and reason of the flesh is death, but the mindset controlled by the Spirit finds life and peace" (Romans 8:6 TPT).

The evil one is an expert at filling our heads with noise and negative chatter. He intentionally ramps it up so we can't think rationally. He wants the noise to distract us from what God is saying. However, he has no authority except what we give him. In order to attack Job, he had to ask permission from God.

GOD KNOWS OUR THOUGHTS

God, however, does know our thoughts. He knows the intents of our hearts, knows what we can take, and what we can't. David said, "You perceive every movement of my heart and soul, and you understand my every thought before it even enters my mind" (Psalms 139:2 TPT).

That's why God said, "Yes," when the devil wanted to test Job. God knew Job would come out even stronger after the testing. God knows so much more than we do and infinitely more than the angels, the devil, and the demons do. We never have to be afraid of the evil one because God will protect us. However, God won't protect us if we don't follow His guidance and leadership. We must obey Him.

His Word is clear on this point. "The person who has My commandments and keeps them is the one who really loves Me; and whoever really loves Me will be loved by My Father, and I will love him and reveal Myself to him. I will make Myself real to him" (John 14:21 AMP).

God also tells us how to differentiate between spirits. "Beloved, do not believe every spirit, but test the spirits, whether they are of God, because many false prophets have gone out into the world. By this you know the Spirit of God: Every spirit that confesses that Jesus Christ has come in the flesh is of God, and every spirit that does not confess that Jesus Christ has come in the flesh is not of God" (I John 4:1-2 NKJV).

THE DEVIL CAN HEAR YOU

The devil and his demons can hear what we say. This can go against us when we say out loud, "I'm so hungry I could eat …" and then we name our favorite treat.

All he has to do is encourage us to eat what we just told him we wanted. In this case, our wish is his command. He will make sure we have what we said we want because he wants to destroy us. Watch what you say.

We can also use this as a weapon against the devil and his demons that mess with our minds. We can mess with theirs. We can actually command them.

Paul told us in Ephesians 2:2-3 TPT, "It wasn't that long ago that you lived in the religion, customs, and values of this world, obeying the dark ruler of the earthly realm who fills the atmosphere with his authority, and works diligently in the hearts of those who are disobedient to the truth of God.

"The corruption that was in us from birth was expressed through the deeds and desires of our self-life. We lived by whatever natural cravings and thoughts our minds dictated,

CHAPTER 12

living as rebellious children subject to God's wrath like everyone else."

Before we became Christians, we were children of disobedience and the devil had power over us. We were in full-fledged rebellion against God and doing whatever we wanted whenever we wanted. It was all dictated by what we craved. This can also happen if we are Christians but choosing to be disobedient.

That's the bad news. Here's the good news. "But God still loved us with such great love. He is so rich in compassion and mercy. Even when we were dead and doomed in our many sins, He united us into the very life of Christ and saved us by His wonderful grace!

"He raised us up with Christ the exalted One, and we ascended with Him into the glorious perfection and authority of the heavenly realm, for we are now co-seated as one with Christ!" (Ephesians 2:4-6 TPT).

At one time we were children of disobedience following our cravings, but now we have the right to become the children of obedience to Jesus Christ our Lord.

CHILDREN OF OBEDIENCE

After reading these verses, I took charge of my life and began to understand how to defeat the enemy at his own game. Now when I sense he is trying to tempt me, I simply address him directly in order to take away his power. I say to him, "No devil, I'm no longer going to listen to you. I am a child of obedience to Jesus Christ my Lord and King. Go away and leave me alone. You have no authority here. In Jesus' mighty name, be gone."

The first time I did this I was a little apprehensive, but I saw a major let up in his temptations. The next time I was bolder, louder, and more direct. His temptations got less overt and more covert, but I was stronger in the Lord and could see with more clarity what the father of lies was trying to do to me.

In John 8:44 NIV, Jesus said, "When he lies, he speaks his native language, for he is a liar and the father of lies."

The devil tries to make his lies prettier by dressing them up as half-truths. A half-truth is still just a lie and will eventually lead me to do what will put me in bondage again. Remember, the devil does not want to help us, he wants to destroy us.

> **The devil tries to make his lies prettier by dressing them up as half-truths.**

So, let's focus on God, His voice, and His plan for us instead of the voice of the enemy. God's plan is really clear when Jesus said, "The thief has only one thing in mind—he wants to steal, slaughter, and destroy. But I have come to give you everything in abundance, more than you expect —life in its fullness until you overflow!" (John 10:10 TPT).

Even though God wants the best for us, He always gives us a choice. He told the Children of Israel in Deuteronomy 30:19-20 NLT, "Today I have given you the choice between life and death, between blessings and curses. Now I call on heaven and earth to witness the choice you make.

"Oh, that you would choose life, so that you and your descendants might live! You can make this choice by loving the Lord your God, obeying Him, and committing yourself firmly to Him. This is the key to your life. And if you love and obey the Lord, you will live long in the land the Lord swore to give your ancestors."

We get mixed up regarding what is good for us, but here Moses gives us two distinct categories. Life is good. Death is bad. Life is blessings. Death is curses. Life is hope. Death is disaster.

God wants us to have an over-the-top, overflowingly full life. The devil just wants to destroy us anyway he can. This brings me to another excuse. If we have all this noise in our heads how can we ever distinguish between God's voice and the devil's? Here are 10 things to help.

TEN THINGS ABOUT GOD'S VOICE

1. He will lead me to the whole truth not a half-truth.

2. He will not violate scripture but will fulfill it.

3. He will lead me towards my destiny not away from it.

4. He will redirect me according to His will, not mine.

5. He will cause me to thin rather than act on impulse.

6. He will never encourage me to fulfill fleshly desires but lead me to fulfill kingdom purposes.

7. He is loving, kind, gentle, soft, and understanding.

8. When I argue with Him, He doesn't argue back. He simply states a truth.

9. He is always speaking to me and speaks out of my experience and understanding.

10. He wants me to know His voice.

TEN THINGS ABOUT THE DEVIL'S VOICE

1. He speaks in half-truths and lies.

2. He violates scripture.

3. He leads me away from my destiny.

4. He helps me do what I want.

5. He wants me to act on impulse and not stop to think.

6. He encourages my indulgences and fleshly desires.

7. He is accusatory, angry, judgmental, and infuses me with guilt, shame, and condemnation.

8. He argues with me and tries to tempt me.

9. The last thing he wants me to do is to understand the motive behind what he's saying.

10. He tries to disguise his voice, so I won't know it's him.

We have two categories life or death. Many times, we don't want to put a thought that enters our minds in one of those extreme categories. We want to put it in the middle, in the gray category, the it-doesn't-matter-this-time category, the one-won't-hurt-me category, or the I-can-eat-just-this-one category. These are all in what we call the gray category, but for a Christian there is no gray category.

We need to face what we are dealing with. We need to intentionally make firm decisions about whether the influences and substances in our lives are good or bad. We must ask questions like, "Is this furthering His kingdom? Is it something God has called me to do? Is it something God wants me to do? Is it within the boundaries God has given me on my healthy living journey?"

CHAPTER 12

YOUR VOICE

The third voice in this noisy mix is your voice. Many of us are listening to so many dissonant voices that we don't even know our own voice. We are opening our ear-gates to everything that comes our way.

Paul said in Romans 10:17 NKJV, "Faith comes by hearing and hearing by the Word of God." Notice it doesn't say faith comes by hearing the Word of God. It delineates the Word of God as the correct thing we should use to guide what we hear.

Everything that comes in through our ear-gate is something we hear. This is why we should guard our hearts. If it's in scripture, we can choose it as a message we can speak over our lives.

> The Holy Spirit should be our gatekeeper because there are too many noisy thoughts in our minds.

"Above all, guard the affections of your heart, for they affect all that you are. Pay attention to your innermost being, for from there flows the wellspring of life" (Proverbs 4:23 TPT).

Our minds lead our wills and emotions. They can help us make the right decisions, but only if they are Holy Spirit-led. This goes deeper than just accepting Christ as our Savior. We still have to make an intentional choice to listen to God.

The Holy Spirit should be our gatekeeper because there are too many noisy thoughts in our minds. We have to learn to categorize those thoughts and take captive the ones that are in the bad category.

"We can demolish every deceptive fantasy that opposes God and break through every arrogant attitude that is raised up in defiance of the true knowledge of God. We capture, like prisoners of war, every thought and insist that it bow in obedience to the Anointed One" (II Corinthians 10:4-7 TPT).

We can willfully choose to allow in the thoughts that are in alignment with what God wants for us. Paul admonished in Philippians 4:8 TPT, "Keep your thoughts continually fixed on all that is authentic and real, honorable and admirable, beautiful and respectful, pure and holy, merciful and kind. And fasten your thoughts on every glorious work of God, praising Him always."

LIFE IS A TRUE-FALSE TEST

In life there are only two choices. You can choose God's truth which brings life, blessings, goodness, future, and hope. Or you can choose the lies of the enemy which brings curses, disaster, destruction, and death. Which do you want to influence your life?

When thoughts come into your mind, categorize them as good or bad, God's truth or the enemy's lies. If you leave it in the gray category, it can still become a guiding factor in your life, but you don't want nebulous thoughts to lead your lives.

We keep those thoughts because we don't know what to do with them, but they are still there. Eventually they will raise their ugly heads and lead us somewhere we don't want to go.

We must be definitive about what God's truth is and what the lies of the enemy are. We do this by aligning our thoughts with God's Word. Then we ask for God to give us wisdom to

CHAPTER 12

follow Him. His wisdom is clear, plain, and simple. He will give us His wisdom if we ask Him.

The only way we can guard against the noise in our minds is to do what God advised. "Step out of the traffic! Take a long, loving look at me, your High God, above politics, above everything" (Psalm 46:10 MSG).

There is a lot of noise in both politics and traffic. The only way to discern what the truth really is, is to put God first and focus on Him and only Him.

When we listen only to God and tune out all the other voices, that's when perfect peace invades our souls.

Remember this, "If it costs you your peace, it's too expensive."

PRAY THIS PRAYER

"Lord Jesus, help me to stop all the noise in my mind. Keep me from doing what You don't want me to do, but what I always seem to go back to.

"Help me take my thoughts captive in obedience to You.

"Don't let my secret, selfish sins control me.

"I desire that the words of my mouth, the thoughts I meditate on, and the intents of my heart always be pure, pleasing and acceptable to You, my only Redeemer, my Protector, my Savior and my Friend.

"In Your name. Amen."

STOP ALL THE NOISE

ANSWER THESE QUESTIONS

1. What voice seems to be yelling the loudest and what is it constantly telling you? Write down everything you can remember.

2. The devil can't read our minds, but what can he do?

3. What stands out to you about the evil one's voice?

4. What stands out to you about God's voice?

CHAPTER 12

5. How has the evil one attacked you, especially in the area of overeating?

6. How can you defeat the devil at his own game?

7. How can you choose what you want to influence your life?

STOP ALL THE NOISE

CHAPTER 12

*"Above all,
guard the affections
of your heart,
for they affect
all that you are
Pay attention to your
innermost being,
for from there flows the
wellspring of life."*

PROVERBS 4:23 TPT

CHAPTER 13

GOD DOESN'T SPEAK TO ME

One of the biggest excuses we have is we feel God doesn't speak to us. This excuse shuts down our ability to hear from Him, trust Him, and surrender to Him. All three of these things are integral when we are trying change our habits, lose weight, get healthy, and follow God's plan for our lives.

When we don't think we have any clear direction from God, we are relying on our own intellect. We may know what to do, but our minds are overridden by our emotions. We say we don't want our emotions to be in charge, but that is like trying to get a two-year-old out of the swimming pool when they want to stay. They cry and scream uncontrollably because they are driven by what they feel.

We aren't quite that demonstrative when we want our way, but we do allow our desires to lead us. When we know what we should eat in order to maintain our health but instead violate our own boundaries, we are abdicating to our fleshly desires which are driven by our emotions.

CHAPTER 13

Paul said in Romans 8:5-6 TPT, "Those who are motivated by the flesh only pursue what benefits themselves. But those who live by the impulses of the Holy Spirit are motivated to pursue spiritual realities. For the sense and reason of the flesh is death, but the mind-set controlled by the Spirit finds life and peace."

Then he gave us the solution. "When the Spirit of Christ empowers your life, you are not dominated by the flesh but by the Spirit. And if you are not joined to the Spirit of the Anointed One, you are not of Him" (Romans 8:9 TPT).

Only the leadership of the Holy Spirit can enable us to crucify our flesh, override our emotionally driven will, and give us the strength to say no and mean it. If we believe God can't or won't speak to us, our ears will be closed to His voice. When that happens, we are on our own. The Holy Spirit is a gentleman. He won't speak to us unless we ask Him to and want His guidance.

HEARD GOD BUT DIDN'T OBEY

That reminds me of a time I heard God clearly and yet, I totally disobeyed Him. It was 1977. I was in my morning quiet time. I had just read Matthew 17:20 NIV where Jesus tells the disciples, "I tell you, if you have faith as small as a mustard seed, you can say to this mountain, 'Move from here to there,' and it will move. Nothing will be impossible for you."

I said out loud, "God, I have a little faith and I have a mountain of weight on my body. How can this mountain be moved?"

I had heard from God before, but this day His voice was clearer than clear. Not verbal but clear in my mind. He said,

"Stop eating sugar. Eat more meats, fruits, and vegetables. And stop eating so much bread."

I knew this was from God for three reasons. First, I cried out to God specifically. Second, I asked a question based on scriptures. Third, it was not something I had ever thought about or heard before.

I wrote down what God said to me. Then I wrote my response. "Nice plan, God. If I did that I would lose weight, but I can't do that."

For the next 30 years, whenever I would get totally frustrated about my weight, I would go on a diet that had some of the elements God had outlined. However, during that time I never did what God actually said which was to stop eating sugar. I heard Him. I knew it was Him. I just refused to do what He said.

> Follow and obey God's voice instead of what you want.

Jesus said, "My sheep hear My voice, and I know them, and they follow Me" (John 10:27 NKJV). I was His. I heard His voice. He knew me as one of His and talked to me, but I did not follow Him. I did not do what He clearly told me to do.

What I've learned is that sometimes God intentionally does not speak anything new to us because we haven't done the last thing He told us to do. We need to do that before He will tell us anything else. He wants to see that we are following Him and obeying His voice instead of what we want.

Other times we pray, but we have our own agendas. We ask God to answer our prayers in our ways, and when He doesn't answer like we want Him to, we think He's not listening to us. He's listening. He just wants to be sure we are too and that we

CHAPTER 13

are following through with what He wants instead of going our own way.

Many times through the years, I'd pray and ask Him what is my purpose? God would give me the answer He gave me back in 1977. I'd get frustrated and say, "I'm not asking about losing weight. I'm asking about what my life purpose is." I was not very nice about it. I was sort-of like the two-year-old having a temper tantrum because I didn't get the answer I wanted. God, though, was always calm and patient with me and gave me the same answer. "Stop eating sugar."

IDENTITY COMES BEFORE PURPOSE

He was helping me understand that I couldn't step into my purpose until I stepped into my identity. I knew from a seminar I had taken in 1994 that was, "I am a whole, healthy, happy woman of God." I was far from that. I had to step into who God said I was before I could even start towards my purpose.

I now know He wanted me to become a Christian weight loss coach, author, speaker, and podcaster with a breaker anointing to help set free those who are being held captive by food addiction. I couldn't do that until I had victory over my biggest obstacle, which was sugar addiction and super morbid obesity.

Today, I can speak with confidence about this subject because I have been through what I can only describe as a living hell. I went from carrying 250 extra pounds on my body to letting God show me how to discard that weight for good. I've been totally free for 10 years.

I know from experience there are times we don't recognize God's voice because we have allowed the voice of our wants and the enemy's voice to cause such noise in our minds that we are too paralyzed to even think of what to say to God. Plus, we assume He isn't interested in talking to us.

Be assured, God wants to have a conversation with us. Many times, my conversations with Him begin with a scripture passage I've read and don't understand. So, I ask Him for clarification.

During the course of my day, I might ask Him for advice on a simple decision, like which way should I take to go home from an appointment? It's so interesting to me that the God of the universe really wants to take time to give me even little bits of direction during my day.

Many times, when I'm driving and listening to a Christian podcast a question from what the speaker says hits me. I pause the podcast, talk with God about it, and He clarifies things for me. It's not my intellect taking over. It is God reminding me of experiences in my life I can draw from to understand a deeper truth.

SOLITUDE AND SILENCE WITH GOD

Some of my favorite times with God are when I just sit in solitude and silence with Him. I have my favorite chair and favorite place to do that. I turn off the lights and any extraneous sounds. I just say, "God, I'm here. What do You want me to know?"

I used to take my questions and my agenda list to Him during my quiet time. Instea,d now I spend time allowing Him to empty my mind of all distractions and tune into what He wants me to know. Sometimes it comes like a moving picture in my mind where God takes me to a beautiful place and we sit and talk.

Sometimes, it's His words reminding me of what I mean to Him. Sometimes, it's just total silence. In the past this would make me anxious to get on with my day, but I feel His presence and know there is nowhere I'd rather be than right there wrapped up in Him.

"You're my place of quiet retreat, and Your wraparound presence becomes my shield as I wrap myself in Your Word!" (Psalm 119:114 TPT). When I leave this time even though I haven't asked Him to give me a to-do list, I know exactly what I need to do next.

Speaking with God should be just like talking to a friend. He doesn't want our opinions as much as He just wants a conversation. He doesn't need us to tell Him what to do. He wants to be our God, our counselor, the One we run to when we are in need.

He wants us to bring our problems to Him, lie them at His feet, and let Him comfort us in the midst of what is going on. He wants us to ask Him things like, "How do I get through this?" We need to do that instead of us telling Him what to do. If it's a health situation, we pray for healing. "Heal, Jesus, according to Your will. Help me get through this time leaning on You."

GOD WILL DIRECT US IF WE LET HIM

We shouldn't try to direct God. We need to let Him direct us. He wants our joy and happiness. If we are in constant conversation with Him, He will guide and direct our steps and keep us from harm.

"The Lord directs the steps of the godly. He delights in every detail of their lives. Though they stumble, they will never fall, for the Lord holds them by the hand" (Psalms 32: 23-24 NLT).

God loves it when we ask Him the right questions. He wants us to confess to Him the lies we are believing and ask Him what His truth is. He loves it when we don't act like we know it all, but we long to hear His voice.

We can be assured He will answer us when we ask questions like: Why am I so afraid? What do you think of me? Who am I? What do You want me to know? These are questions that capture God's attention. Questions that are on our minds. Questions that He longs to answer but won't unless we ask because He is a gentleman.

THE VOICE OF GOD

Psalms 119 is known as a chapter that tells is about the voice of God, which is also embodied in His written Word. Listen to these dynamic words of God.

"Give me revelation about the meaning of Your ways so I can enjoy the reward of following them fully. Give me an understanding heart so that I can passionately know and obey Your truth. Guide me into the paths that please You, for I take delight in all that You say" (Psalms 119: 33-35 TPT).

"I will walk with You in complete freedom, for I seek to follow Your every command ... My passion and delight is in Your word, for I love what You say to me!" (Psalms 119: 45, 47 TPT).

CHAPTER 13

"I've learned that there is nothing perfect in this imperfect world except Your words, for they bring such fantastic freedom into my life!" (Psalms 119: 96 TPT).

WHAT DOES GOD'S VOICE SOUND LIKE?

Elijah got a lesson directly from God about the sound of God's voice. He had a great victory over the 450 Prophets of Baal, but he became afraid of Queen Jezebel, so he ran away. He was hiding in a cave when God told him to go out and stand on the mountain before Him.

"And behold, the Lord passed by, and a great and strong wind tore into the mountains and broke the rocks in pieces before the Lord, but the Lord was not in the wind; and after the wind an earthquake, but the Lord was not in the earthquake; and after the earthquake a fire, but the Lord was not in the fire; and after the fire a still small voice.

"So it was, when Elijah heard it, that he wrapped his face in his mantle and went out and stood in the entrance of the cave. Suddenly a voice came to him, and said, 'What are you doing here, Elijah?'" (I Kings 19:11-13 NKJV).

God had to shake Elijah out of his funk and discontent. God stopped him by reminding him of what His voice sounds like. God's voice wasn't the loud, angry voice that tore things up. It wasn't like the rushing wind. It wasn't like an earthquake. It wasn't like a fire. It was, and still is, a still, small voice. We have to listen for that voice.

God's voice, though, can be emphatic when He wants us to get what He's saying. It these cases, God may have to raise His voice to make sure we are listening. God has definitely raised

His voice so I could hear Him, been emphatic, and spoken sternly to me. He has to do that with me because I will admit I can be pretty stubborn when I get something in my head.

There was the time when I adamantly refused to go to a writer's conference when I was working on my first book, *Sweet Grace*. I was stuck in the writing process. I'd already been to many writer's conferences. I felt I knew how to write, and my pride told me that going to yet another conference and spending yet more money wasn't necessary.

God finally got my attention after saying my name twice. This time I actually heard someone say my name, but there was no one there. When I acknowledged I was listening, God said, "What if I planned a writer's conference 10 miles from your home and you won't go because of pride?" I went even though I wasn't happy about it. Now after writing seven books and two study guides, I see how pivotal that conference was to my purpose.

God wasn't angry with me, but He was direct. He had something He wanted me to do and He wanted to be sure I did it.

GOD SPEAKS TRUTH AND PEACE

One way we know how to recognize God's voice is that He always speaks the truth. "God also bound Himself with an oath, so that those who received the promise could be perfectly sure that He would never change His mind. So, God has given both His promise and His oath. These two things are unchangeable because it is impossible for God to lie. Therefore, we who have fled to Him for refuge can have great confidence as we hold to the hope that lies before us" (Hebrews 6:17-18 NLT).

CHAPTER 13

God's voice speaks peace. No other voice does this like His. "I listen carefully to what God the Lord is saying, for He speaks peace to His faithful people" (Psalms 85:8 NLT).

Then He declared, "All who listen to Me will live in peace, untroubled by fear of harm" (Proverbs 1:33 NLT).

There is so much more about God's voice, but the main thing is God does speak to us. He speaks from His Word. He speaks to us through others. He speaks to us through situations and circumstances we find ourselves in. He speaks to us in our minds in a still, small voice.

He even speaks audibly like Samuel experienced. "Then the Lord came and stood and called as at the previous times, 'Samuel! Samuel!' Then Samuel answered, 'Speak, for Your servant is listening'" (II Samuel 3:10 AMP).

Are you ready to hear from God?

PRAY THIS PRAYER

"Lord Jesus, Speak to me. I am one of Your sheep. I am Your servant. I long to hear Your voice.

"Speak to me, Lord. I am listening. I need direction. I need encouragement. I need comfort. I need to know You are with me.

"Speak, Lord, and I will listen and obey.

"In Your name. Amen."

ANSWER THESE QUESTIONS

1. How can we live by the impulses of the Holy Spirit instead of our own desires? See Romans 8:5-6, 9 TPT.

2. When has God told you to do something and you disobeyed or rebelled. Journal about why you did that and what you will do next time He asks you to do something.

3. Why does it seem God sometimes doesn't answer your prayers? Choose the one you think applies to you the most and journal about it.

a. I haven't done the last thing He asked me to do.

b. I am asking something that isn't in God's will.

c. I have so much noise in my mind I can't hear Him.

4. What does God's voice sound like? See I Kings 19:11-13 NKJV.

CHAPTER 13

5. What does your time with God consist of? How often do you meet with Him? What do you do during that time? What can you do to improve it?

6. Has God ever told you emphatically to do something? Did you do it right away? Did you do it later? Did you ignore Him? Journal about that.

7. Does God speak to people today audibly like He did in I Samuel 3:10 AMP? Has He spoken audibly to you or someone you know? What was that like? Do you want Him to speak to you or would it frighten you? Journal about that.

CHAPTER 13

*"You're my place
of quiet retreat,
and Your wraparound
presence becomes
my shield
as I wrap myself
in Your Word!"*

PSALMS 119:114 TPT

CHAPTER 14

DO I HAVE A VOICE?

To say we have no voice or no say in what happens in our lives is an excuse for not surrendering to the Holy Spirit. It means we are just living by every whim we have and not by faith in God. However, we do have a voice.

Our voices will be dynamically powerful, marked by continuous productive activity and changed in an energetic way when we make sure we have left behind our desires and cravings which seem to lead us down the wrong paths.

"As you yield to the dynamic life and power of the Holy Spirit, you will abandon the cravings of your self-life" (Galatians 5:16 TPT).

With so many other voices competing for our attention, it can be difficult to hear our own voice. That makes us feel we don't have any input into our own lives.

However, God made us with a soul, which we understand to be comprised of our minds, wills, and emotions. Not only that, but He made us with vocal cords so that we can speak, sing, preach, and pray. We have a voice, but many times we

CHAPTER 14

feel that voice has been stolen from us and we are afraid to speak up lest what we say will be shot down.

This happens many times when we are children and our parents or teachers have not allowed us to speak. We've been told we can be seen but not heard. We have to be quiet at home, quiet at school, quiet when adults are talking, and especially quiet at church.

As an adult we feel we don't have anything to contribute. We stay quiet so we won't be challenged, called out or made fun of. God, however, made you with a unique voice. Did you know that no two voices are the same? DNA has proven this is true. God made each of us with a unique sound and a unique perspective.

GOD LONGS TO HEAR YOUR VOICE

Remember when Adam and Eve sinned. and they hid themselves from God. God asked Adam, "Where are you?" (Genesis 3:9 NLT). God knew where Adam and Eve were, but He wanted to hear their voices. He wanted to have a conversation with them. It wasn't a conversation that praised them, but still God had wanted to hear what they had to say.

God created us. "All things were created by Him and for Him" (Colossians 1:16 NLT). We were created for God. Not only that, but He created each of us individually with three distinct parts.

"Now may the God of peace make you holy in every way, and may your whole spirit and soul and body be kept blameless until our Lord Jesus Christ comes again" (I Thessalonians 5:23 NLT).

We know our bodies are the physical part of us. We know our spirit is the part of us that connects to God's Spirit. The soul is the part of us that is sometimes difficult to understand. "God formed Man out of dirt from the ground and blew into his nostrils the breath of life. The Man came alive—a living soul" (Genesis 2:7 MSG).

WHAT IS THE SOUL?

The construct of our souls is important in understanding who we are and what our voice is. Most Biblical scholars agree the soul is composed of three parts: the mind, will, and emotions.

Our voice, or the essence of who we are, resides in our souls. It is a combination of what we think in our minds, what we decide in our wills, and what we feel through our emotions.

Scripture explains knowledge is a part of our souls. This indicates our minds are part of our souls. "When wisdom enters your heart, and knowledge is pleasant to your soul, discretion will preserve you; understanding will keep you" (Proverbs 2:10-11 NKJV).

Our souls remember. Our minds are the part of our souls where we remember things. "My soul still remembers" (Lamentations 3:10 NKJV).

Our wills, which are where decisions are made, are also a part of our souls. Job 7:15 speaks of the soul choosing and Job 6:7 speaks of the soul refusing. Both of these indicate making decisions.

In the Old Testament, God told the people they needed to make a decision to serve Him "with all their hearts and souls"

CHAPTER 14

(Deuteronomy 10:12 NLT). This is another reference to our wills, as well.

Our emotions are also a component of our souls, and many times drive our voices. Emotions like love, joy, and many others reside in our souls.

"Tell me, You whom my soul loves" (Song of Solomon 1:7 ESV). It is with our souls that we love God. "You shall love the Lord your God with all your heart and with all your soul and with all your might" (Deuteronomy 6:5 ESV).

It is also in our souls that the emotion of joy is felt. "Make the soul of Your servant joyful, for to You, Lord, I lift up my soul" (Psalm 86:4 NASB).

There are many more scriptures that reveal the nature of the soul, but these lay the groundwork to help us understand all that is uniquely us resides in our souls or our minds, wills, and emotions. or our thoughts, decisions, and feelings.

UNIQUELY YOU

Your voice is uniquely you. When it partners with the voice of God, it becomes a powerhouse that can send the devil running. He hates your Spirit-led voice whether it is the spoken or written word because He hates the truth.

Embrace your voice. It can be a powerful force, especially if we use it to tie the hands of the evil one. There is a problem with our voices, though, if we speak out of our fleshly desires or out of our soulish nature without the Spirit of God.

Jesus talked a lot about this. "If anyone wishes to follow Me, he must deny himself, set aside selfish interests, and take up his cross and follow Me. For whoever wishes to save his life will lose it, but whoever loses his life for My sake will find it" (Matthew 16:24-25 AMP).

Jesus also said our selfish interests or soulish desires must be set aside in order to follow Him. When He said those of us who wish to save our lives will lose it, He was talking about us only being concerned about things in this world, our desires, and cravings.

These are things we have decided we need. We have rationalized those wants and are emotionally attached to them, as if they were needs. However, if we do this Jesus said, we will lose our physical lives.

He added if we put aside selfish desires and make the choice to give them up or lose them, we will find life with Jesus for all eternity.

Then He continued, "For what will it profit a man if he gains the whole world, wealth, fame, success, but forfeits his soul? Or what will a man give in exchange for his soul?" (Matthew 16:26 AMP).

> When we lose our souls, we lose the essence of who we are. When we partner with Father God, Jesus, and the Holy Spirit we will find true life.

When we lose our souls, we lose the essence of who we are. When we partner with Father God, Jesus, and the Holy Spirit we will find true life. This is a huge key to finding our true voice as a child of the King.

I have had two distinct voices. Before I began my transformation journey, my voice was driven by my soulish desires, which included overeating to calm my emotions. The emotional part of my soul governed my life. My feelings

CHAPTER 14

overrode my decisions. I had formed such bad habits that my mind seemed like it was being reasonable when it agreed I could and should eat whatever I wanted.

I was a Christian, regular church attender, even taught adult Sunday School classes, but I was allowing my humanity to steer my soul where food was concerned. I had not yet surrendered that part of my life.

I was living by Romans 7. "For I know that nothing good lives within the flesh of my fallen humanity. The longings to do what is right are within me, but willpower is not enough to accomplish it. My lofty desires to do what is good are dashed when I do the things I want to avoid" (Romans 7:18-19 TPT).

> The emotional part of my soul governed my life. My feelings overrode my decisions.

Paul continued his explanation in Romans 7:22-23 TPT, "Truly, deep within my true identity, I love to do what pleases God. But I discern another power operating in my humanity, waging a war against the moral principles of my conscience, and bringing me into captivity as a prisoner to the law of sin—this unwelcome intruder in my humanity."

Then he asked the pivotal question I finally asked myself. "Oh, what a miserable person I am! Who will free me from this life that is dominated by sin and death?" (Romans 7:24 NLT).

I had a voice, but it wasn't the right voice and I knew that. My voice was being overridden by the voice of the enemy and my selfish desires. The next verse explained to me how the yoke of sin could be broken in my lie. "Thank God! The answer is in Jesus Christ our Lord" (Romans 7:25 NLT).

My soul knew what I needed. I needed to embrace all of Jesus, not just the part I was OK with. When the monumental shift finally happened in my life, my voice began to change. When I realized I was being controlled by substances that were harmful to me, I finally fully submitted my soul, the essence of who I am, to God. That changed my voice completely.

> When the monumental shift happened in my life, my voice began to change!

I began to understand my voice has to speak from my mind which I had to allow God to renew. "Therefore, I urge you, brothers and sisters, in view of God's mercy, to offer your bodies as a living sacrifice, holy and pleasing to God—this is your true and proper worship. Do not conform to the pattern of this world but be transformed by the renewing of your mind. Then you will be able to test and approve what God's will is—His good, pleasing, and perfect will" (Romans 12:1-2 NIV).

The renewing of my mind had to come by me fixing my attention on God and not on what I decided, felt, or thought. I had to make a willful decision based on what I knew was true for me. I did not want to continue to be super morbidly obese. Only by offering my body as a living sacrifice could I make that shift.

I had to take "my everyday ordinary life, my sleeping, eating, going-to-work and walking-around life and place it before God as an offering" (Romans 12:1 MSG). It wasn't easy,

CHAPTER 14

but with, by, and through God's strength I was able to lose the weight and work at keeping it off.

I didn't have a strong voice before, even in my writing. I was trying to find it, but it really didn't happen until I finally did what God had been asking me to do for years. I surrendered the foods I loved to Him.

That's when I found my voice. I didn't know it, but God did. He called me to write my first book. Then He called me to use my voice in a different way through group coaching, one-on-one coaching, and speaking on Christian television and radio shows.

Then, in October of 2019, God was adamant I needed to start a podcast. I had no idea how or why. It all came together in a month and the first episode was released. Then 2020 happened and all speaking engagements stopped. Everything went online. God knew that in advance. Now, I love doing podcasts because I am no longer afraid of using my voice.

WHAT COMPRISES YOUR VOICE?

There are several things that comprise our voices. We speak from our souls. We speak from the gifts, talents, and abilities that God has given us. Some sing, some write poetry, some paint pictures, some are great speakers, some have a gift of prayer, prophecy, or encouragement. Some are like me and love writing. It all depends on how God has gifted, called, and anointed you.

Our voices will be influenced by all of our experiences, both good and bad, everything we have learned, every job we've had, every person we've allowed to speak into our lives. Our voices will also be influenced by our personalities and what we are passionate about.

Our voices grow out of our identity and point us towards our destinies. My identity is I am a whole, healthy, happy woman administering grace and truth in a powerful way energized by the Holy Spirit. I am living out my destiny right now because I finally learned I do have a voice. It is meant to be used for whatever purpose God wants me to use it.

God has a purpose for each of us. "We have become His poetry, a re-created people that will fulfill the destiny He has given each of us, for we are joined to Jesus, the Anointed One. Even before we were born, God planned in advance our destiny and the good works we would do to fulfill it!" (Ephesians 2:10 TPT).

JOINED TO JESUS

We must be joined to Jesus before we can even begin to think about our destinies or fulfilling them. In order to do that we have to know who we are. Your identity has to come before your purpose.

For many years I struggled with my identity. I knew back in 1994, God had revealed to me that who He wanted me to be was a whole, healthy, happy woman. For most of my adult life I was far from it. I couldn't even see that as a prophecy which might come true someday.

I didn't have any faith it would ever happen because I had tried everything to lose weight. I'd lose it and then just gain it back again because I didn't listen to God's voice. I didn't want to commit to what I knew would be a monumental change.

CHAPTER 14

God, though, had other plans. He wanted faith in Him to become part of my voice. "Now faith brings our hopes into reality and becomes the foundation needed to acquire the things we long for. It is all the evidence required to prove what is still unseen" (Hebrews 11:1 TPT).

I had hoped I would lose weight, but it was more like wishful thinking. To have my hopes turn into reality seemed like a pipedream to me, but not to God. When I took the first risky step of faith not knowing where my foot would fall, I didn't have evidence what God was placing in my heart would ever become a reality.

I knew that if I kept doing what I had always done, I'd get what I'd always gotten, which was a larger and larger body. I placed my faith in God, not in myself because I didn't trust myself or my voice. I put my trust in God.

He was my last resort because I knew "without faith living within us it would be impossible to please God. For we come to God in faith knowing that He is real and that He rewards the faith of those who passionately seek Him" (Hebrews 11:6 TPT).

REPENTANCE EQUALS BLUBBERING

My seeking looked more like blubbering and crying as I repented of what I had done to the body God had given me. We can't make any decisions without the guidance of the Holy Spirit.

We can't have any thoughts that really lead our lives unless we have allowed Jesus to renew our minds. We can't trust our emotions unless we first pour them out to Father God and leave them with Him.

Then our souls will be led by God. Then He will help us find our true voice that will always speak the truth in love. "Speaking the truth in love, we will grow to become in every respect the mature body of Him who is the head, that is, Christ" (Ephesians 4:15 NIV).

Did you know that God actually delights in you? He loves to hear your voice and see how you live. "The Lord directs the steps of the godly. He delights in every detail of their lives" (Psalms 27:23 NLT).

The question is not do you have a voice. Undeniably you do. The real question is, "What leads your voice?" Is it your selfish desires or the Spirit of God?

PRAY THIS PRAYER

"Holy Spirit, I long to have my soul led by Your Spirit and Your Spirit only. I just don't know how to set aside some of the things I think I can't live without.

"I know these are things that are led by my feelings which affect my decisions and impact my thoughts. Help me to discard the things that are making me lose my soul.

"Help me find the voice You want me to have. I submit to You and only You. Show me what You want for my life.

"In Jesus' name. Amen."

CHAPTER 14

ANSWER THESE QUESTIONS

1. What does God mean if He asks you, "Where are you?"

2. What are the three distinct parts of our souls and what do they govern?

3. What does Matthew 16:24-26 AMP tell us that impacts all of our lives?

4. How can we have two different voices?

5. What does Romans 12:1-2 tell us we must do to have the right kind of voice?

6. Why is faith instrumental in finding our voices and our destinies?

7. Journal about what this quote means to you. "We can't make any decisions without the guidance of the Holy Spirit. We can't have any thoughts that really lead our lives unless we have allowed Jesus to renew our minds. We can't trust our emotions unless we first pour them out on Father God."

CHAPTER 14

CHAPTER 15

TOO OLD TO EAT HEALTHY

Are you too old to eat healthy? When I asked people what their excuses were for not losing weight and getting healthy one excuse that came up often was, I am too old to lose weight. One woman said, "I don't have long at my age, so why not enjoy what's left?" That made me feel sad for her because if the only enjoyment we are getting out of life is eating, then we need to re-examine our lives.

As I look back over my life, though, there was at least 30 years where food was my main enjoyment. Going out to eat was entertainment. Fixing a big dinner and having my family and friends over was how we had a good time. Fixing a special dessert was something fun to do. Baking cookies with my daughter reminded me of the good old days when I baked cookies with Grandma.

The problem was that overeating was a very destructive type of entertainment for me. I got to the point where eating huge amounts of my favorites garnered me a death sentence. I wasn't ready for such a pronouncement. It was the first time

CHAPTER 15

I realized that I played a role in my own life expectancy. Of course, anything can happen to us at any time, but that day I realized I needed to do something about my weight. It took a while, but I realized I am too old not to eat healthy.

This year I turned 69. I have always hated the years ending in nines because they mark the end of a decade. The years since 59, though, have been some of the best years of my life. I am so glad that I lost the weight. Even though I was older when I did it, my weight loss, writing books, coaching, speaking, and podcasting have taken me places I would have never dreamed of when I was 19.

GOD'S HAND IN EVERYTHING

When I look back over my life, I see God's hand in everything I've been through. It would have been great if I hadn't gained so much weight, but if I never gained the weight, I would have never realized how I needed to surrender to God. I would have never walked through one of the hardest times in my life and I would never have been able to help those who are where I once was to get out of their pit of despair.

I see how at every point God was leading me. He was never on my timeline, but I was always on His. He was working in my life for good to happen and for His design for me to be fulfilled, no matter what age I have been. "We are convinced that every detail of our lives is continually woven together for good, for we are His lovers who have been called to fulfill His designed purpose" (Romans 8:28 TPT).

One great thing about getting older is the value of the wisdom that comes with age. I'm sorry, but it is just not wisdom to say that eating whatever you want and not paying attention to your health is a wise thing when you get older.

Things will happen to our bodies when we get older because they are not designed to last as long as we'd like them to. Even though we humans have come up with replacement parts, like knees and hearts, they are still not up to par with the original parts. Our bodies will wear out.

It's up to us, no matter what age we are, to make our health a priority. If we want to know if that is true or not, we need only ask God. He promises to give us wisdom if we ask. "If any of you lacks wisdom, you should ask God, who gives generously to all without finding fault, and it will be given to you" (James 1:5 TPT).

David said, "Help us to remember that our days are numbered and help us to interpret our lives correctly. Set Your wisdom deeply in our hearts so that we may accept Your correction" (Psalms 90:12 TPT).

GOD IS WATCHING

God is watching what we are doing. We don't get a pass to overindulge in our selfish desires just because we've lived a little longer. If anything, we are required to be role models to others.

"The Lord looks over us from where He rules in heaven. Gazing into every heart from His lofty dwelling place, He observes all the peoples of the earth. The Creator of our hearts considers and examines everything we do" (Psalms 33:13-15 TPT). This is very similar to another Old Testament verse. "The eyes of the Lord search the whole earth in order to strengthen

CHAPTER 15

those whose hearts are fully committed to Him" (II Chronicles 16:9 NLT).

He's not watching so He can chastise us. He is watching so He can strengthen us, empower us, and anoint us. When we are in service to Him, when our hearts are fully committed to Him, God has an overwhelming desire to continue to bring blessings and opportunities into our lives.

If I hadn't finally done what God wanted me to do, which was to make Him my Lord rather than the foods I loved, I know I would be dead today. I would have missed out on what God had planned for me from the beginning of time.

COACHING WAS NEVER ON MY LIST

Even though I am retired, I spend a lot of my time coaching Overcomers Academy members about how to work with God to transform their lifestyles. Many days I feel like I am living in a dream world. I love what I am doing. However, coaching and helping others lose weight was never at the top of my want-to list. As a writer, the main thing I wanted to do was write a book about someone who had done something great with God's help.

Number 1, I never knew the book would be about me. Even when I lost 250 pounds, I didn't feel I'd done anything special. After all, I failed miserably in order to have to lose that amount of weight.

Number 2, I never thought I was someone who could do something great. I mean, when you weigh 430 pounds there is a lot of self-hatred that gets dragged into the mix. I knew God had given me a writing gift, but that's where any good thing in me ended.

Number 3, I didn't like speaking. I had no idea that writing a popular book would mean I'd be on national and international Christian television and radio. I didn't know it would mean I would be doing a weekly 30-minute podcast. Yet, God is faithful and always reveals to me what to say. His presence is truly the highlight of everything I do. God always knew I would be doing every one of those things.

> What if I had just said, "I want to enjoy my remaining years swimming in sugar?"

I did all of this after age 59. I lost the weight right before that, but all the rest has happened in the last 10 years. What if I had never taken the time to lose the weight? What if I had said, "I just want to enjoy my remaining years swimming in sugar?"

It's difficult for us to understand that overindulging in food could be considered ungodly. After all, it's something many of us do at a church potluck dinner. We are supposed to be fellowshipping with others. Instead many times we are seeing how fast we can get to the dessert table.

Paul delineated many of the things we do that are against what God wants for us in Galatians 5:19-21 WEY. "Now you know full well the doings of our lower natures. Fornication, impurity, indecency, idol-worship, sorcery, enmity, strife, jealousy, outbursts of anger, intrigues, dissensions, factions, envying, hard drinking, riotous feasting, and the like. And as to these I forewarn you, as I have already forewarned you, that those who are guilty of such things will have no share in the Kingdom of God." This translation uses the words riotous feasting instead of orgies. Perhaps they are kin to each other.

In this same chapter, Paul gives us the cure for gluttony or any of the other cravings we might have. "Let your lives be guided by the Spirit, and then you will certainly not indulge the cravings of your lower natures. For the cravings of the lower nature are opposed to those of the Spirit, and the cravings of the Spirit are opposed to those of the lower nature; because these are antagonistic to each other, so that you cannot do everything to which you are inclined" (Galatians 5:16-17 WEY).

This is wisdom and those of us who are older should be putting on our wisdom hats and understanding that just because overeating may be something we consider fun, it doesn't mean it is something God says is OK. It still has the possibility of damaging our bodies. Many diseases are exacerbated by overindulging in food. It may seem harmless, but it is not.

Food can and should be medicine if it is the right kind of food in the right quantity. Eat for your health and it can bring you the pleasure you desire.

NEVER TOO OLD TO LOSE WEIGHT

You are never too old to lose weight. The saying that an old dog can't learn new tricks may seem true, but many times we old dogs can learn quicker because we know our Master has our best interests at heart.

While it's true we have a lifetime of habits to sort through, we also know what our bad habits have done to us. Change should be something we long for instead of something we dread.

It's wisdom to understand just because the world around us is doing something, we don't need to do the same thing. Just because everyone else is chowing down and eating whatever they want doesn't mean we should. We are old enough and wise enough to do what God wants us to do, not what the world encourages us to do.

Paul said, "Be very careful how you live, not being like those with no understanding, but live honorably with true wisdom, for we are living in evil times. Take full advantage of every day as you spend your life for His purposes" (Ephesians 5:15 TPT).

IT'S WISDOM TO TRUST GOD

It's wisdom to trust God. Our opinions can easily be swayed, but if we know better, we will do better. "Trust in the Lord completely, and do not rely on your own opinions. With all your heart rely on Him to guide you, and He will lead you in every decision you make. Don't think for a moment that you know it all, for wisdom comes when you adore Him with undivided devotion and avoid everything that's wrong" (Proverbs 3:5-7 TPT).

The Word of God applied to our experiences brings us wisdom. "Let the word of Christ live in you richly, flooding you with all wisdom. Apply the Scriptures as you teach and instruct one another with the Psalms, and with festive praises, and with prophetic songs given to you spontaneously by the Spirit, so sing to God with all your hearts!" (Colossians 3:16 TPT).

Sometimes we are tempted to just throw caution to the wind and do whatever we want. This is never a good idea, especially where overindulging in food is concerned. "The naïve demonstrate a lack of wisdom, but the lovers of wisdom are crowned with revelation-knowledge" (Proverbs 4:18 TPT).

CHAPTER 15

Some of my favorite verses let us know that the foods, which contain an overload of sweetness, really aren't true sweetness. "When God fulfills your longings, sweetness fills your soul" (Proverbs 13:19 TPT). Then in Proverbs 3:17 TPT, Solomon said, "The ways of wisdom are sweet, always drawing you into the place of wholeness."

In our older years, wisdom and wholeness are things we should be following after. We need to allow God to fulfill our true longings. I had no idea that for me that was coaching, podcasting, and speaking. I knew it was writing, but I had no idea about the others. I dearly love seeing people get breakthroughs. It fills my bucket like nothing else. It is true sweetness for me.

> Never too old to eat healthy.

Likewise, it was true wisdom for me to follow what God told me to do in regard to my eating. Even though I thought I could never give up sugar and flour, God showed me how and that led me to become a whole person—body, soul, and spirit. I thought it was just my body that was out of alignment, but it was every part of me because I was not allowing God to be my God.

True wisdom comes from only one source. It comes from God. "All wisdom comes from the Lord, and so do common sense and understanding. God gives helpful advice to everyone who obeys Him and protects those who live as they should" (Proverbs 2:6-7 CEV).

Getting older is not that bad when wisdom comes along with it. I've lived long enough that I am absolutely sure the next great thing God has in store for me and you is just around the corner. I can't wait to see what it is. We are never too old to begin to eat healthy. That's wisdom.

PRAY THIS PRAYER

"Father God, Give me wisdom. I'm certainly old enough. Show me the ways I am not applying Your wisdom to my life and health.

"Make me not afraid to change my habits.

"Give me direction. Give me wisdom. Let me keep my eyes on You alone.

"In Jesus' name. Amen."

ANSWER THESE QUESTIONS

1. Is it wise, no matter how old you are, to eat whatever you want, whenever you want it? Why or why not?

2. When you look back over your life, what are some of the ways you see how God used the good and the bad to get you where He wanted you to be?

3. Why is it important especially for those who are older to eat healthy?

CHAPTER 15

4. How can you be a role model for others in what and how you eat and cook?

5. How can healthy food be some of the best medicine and unhealthy foods lead us to an early grave?

6. What is riotous feasting? Do you ever engage in anything similar to that?

7. How is eating healthy part of Godly wisdom?

TOO OLD TO EAT HEALTHY

CHAPTER 15

"For the eyes of the Lord search the whole earth in order to strengthen those whose hearts are fully committed to Him."

II CHRONICLES 16:9 NLT

CHAPTER 16

NO DIET WORKS FOR ME

Sometimes an excuse we have for not losing weight will lead us to the correct way to lose weight. This is true of the excuse I had, and many others have—no diet works for me.

This was more than an excuse for me. It was the truth. No diet worked for me because I always treated it as a short-term fix for what I knew in my heart was a long-term problem. I wanted to think my obsession with overeating certain foods was something I could overcome with a simple diet, special kind of weight loss pill, or some new pre-packaged diet foods.

I tried everything and nothing worked for me to lose the weight and keep it off. I felt doomed to a life of super morbid obesity, which I knew was going to be a short life if I couldn't figure out how to lose weight and keep it off. The question was, "How do I do that without dieting." The answer eluded me.

According to everyone I knew, everything I had read, and everything any doctor had told me, a diet was the only way I could lose weight. I kept knocking on every new diet door that came along. I could lose weight on diets because I had pretty good willpower, but that would only last for six to nine months. I'd lose 100 pounds. Then, I'd celebrate by eating something made with sugar and flour. That would take me right back to eating like I had before and gaining more weight than I had just taken off.

That's because diets are designed to help us lose weight, then go on a maintenance program. That allows us to eat more food than we did on the diet, but less than we did before dieting. For a sugar and food addict like me, this never helped me change my habits. I just went back to how I had habitually used food to try to solve my problems.

WHY DIETS DON'T WORK

Diet programs don't work to keep the weight off, but they are still popular. This is disconcerting to me because I now know that habit change is the only way to lose weight and keep it off.

Diet programs make their money from return customers. I'm raising my hand here because I returned to the diet program I was most successful on many times. Each time I spent thousands of dollars taking weight off only to put it back on again and add more to it. In other words, dieting made me fatter.

The reason I couldn't stay with it was because it greatly limited my food choices and kept me to under 1,000 calories a day. This is not good for anyone. It did help me lose weight, but I felt starved the entire time. I couldn't wait to reach my goal so I could go off the diet and celebrate by eating cake.

This was before I understood that sugar is very addictive to me. I had not given it up for good. I would just set it aside for the time I was on a diet. I looked forward to being off the diet because I would go back to eating what I craved.

I thought sugar helped me manage my emotions. It did not. It only masked my emotions and then I would need more to help me pretend those feelings weren't there. It was an endless cycle. It was all because I was afraid to be human and feel any emotion that might make me rip-roaring angry or crying buckets of tears in despondency.

I had grown up trying to mask my emotions. I saw others who allowed their emotions to rule their lives, which I did not want for myself.

I wanted my mind to lead me. That seemed like the rational thing to do. I didn't realize that my mind was clouded and ruled by my emotions. Even though it felt like I was making good decisions, my emotions were really overriding both my thoughts and my decisions.

> I saw myself not as happy but as a big, fat blob and regularly told myself that was what I was.

Finally, I just gave up and resigned myself to be fat and happy. However at 430 pounds, I was not happy, not in the least. I had multiple diseases—congestive heart failure, high blood pressure, diabetes, and could barely walk.

I saw myself not as happy but as a big, fat blob and regularly told myself that's what I was. This only made me feel worse, which triggered my emotions to tell my mind and my will that I needed something sweet to eat. I carried my own stash with me everywhere I went. I never wanted to be without my drug of choice.

CHAPTER 16

Then a rude cardiac surgeon told me I had five years to live if I didn't lose at least 100 pounds and keep it off. He was the first person to tell me my future was in my own hands.

It was in the choices I was making. It was in what I ate and what I didn't eat. I was treating the foods I loved like a lifeline, but they were really a tool the enemy was using to destroy me.

For the first time I asked myself, is there a different way to lose weight? If so, what is it? All I ever knew was going on a diet. Even though I knew I could never lose weight and keep it off on diets, I still went back on another diet.

The same thing happened again. This worried me because I was fast approaching the cardiac surgeon's deadline for my expiration.

GOD HAD OTHER PLANS

I am so glad God had other plans. He placed me in a meeting when a mentor of mine made an off-handed statement. "Alcohol is one molecule away from sugar. Alcohol is liquid sugar."

That's all it took. I saw all the pieces of my life come together like a magnetic puzzle. The heavens seemed to open, and I realized what my issue was. I was like an alcoholic only with sugar. To get free of the weight I was carrying I was going to have to figure out how to stop eating sugar.

God had told me to stop eating sugar and flour, but I had ignored Him because I felt I couldn't stop eating those things altogether. Everything I ate seemed to have those as part of the ingredients. How could I stop eating all the great foods I grew up with?

The moment I heard the connection between sugar and alcohol, I knew I was a sugar addict. I had never heard the term used, but I knew I was one, even if I was the only person on the planet who was one.

I also knew I needed to get sugar out of my life for good. It seemed like an impossible task. I was drawn to sugar like a moth is drawn to a flame. Sugar was clearly killing me, but how could I ever stop eating it altogether? It seemed like it was a part of my identity.

To say I needed help is an understatement. Thankfully my mentor started a group for those who had any kinds of problems with addictive behaviors.

I was surprised to learn that addiction of any kind can be overcome in two distinct steps. First, know why you want to overcome whatever you are addicted to. Second, learn how to change your habits. Both were keys for me.

I finally wanted to change. I finally saw sugar for what it was doing to my body. I had started eating it as something to help me anesthetize my pain and emotions. However, it had become a stronghold.

> Sugar was clearly killing me, but how could I ever stop eating it altogether?

The only way to break that stronghold was to surrender sugar to God. It was a difficult process, but when God convicted me that sugar had become like a god to me, I was finally willing to let Him show me how to let it go.

I wanted transformation, but I wanted it to be quick and easy. That's what all the diets promised. Just eat like this and you'll lose the weight you want to lose. While that is true, they

CHAPTER 16

didn't promise me that I could keep the weight off. I wasn't transforming if I was just gaining the weight back. I was going backwards by gaining more weight.

Transformation, though, is not possible without my mind being renewed. I had programmed it a certain way for way too many years. My habits were firmly ingrained and to change them seemed impossible.

In Romans 12:2 NIV Paul told us we can be transformed. In order to make this change, we have to allow God to renew our minds. Romans 12:2 MSG helped me understand in a practical sense what I needed to do. "Fix your attention on God. You'll be changed from the inside out."

> If God was my only focus, I could be changed, transformed, and remade from the inside out.

I realized if God was my only focus, I could be changed, transformed, and remade from the inside out. I had always concentrated on the outside of me since that's what seemed to be my biggest problem area.

I had never really asked God to help me lose weight only to bless any diet I ran across. I realized He couldn't bless the diets because He had already told me I needed to stop eating sugar. I just couldn't figure out how to do that when no diet worked for me.

I accepted the truth that I can't have any type of change in my physical appearance until I have an entire spiritual transformation. I never knew I needed that. I thought God and I were best friends. He was that to me, but I was not living up to my part of the relationship.

I admitted to God that I had amassed the weight that was on my body. I had desecrated the place He considered His temple. I cried. I mourned. I wept. I surrendered my life and my addictions to Him. I had rebelled against Him and sinned because I had not done what He told me to do.

What David said in Psalms became my heart-cry: "God, give me mercy from Your fountain of forgiveness! I know Your abundant love is enough to wash away my guilt. Because Your compassion is so great, take away this shameful guilt of sin. Forgive the full extent of my rebellious ways, and erase this deep stain on my conscience" (Psalms 51:1-2 TPT).

I wanted a changed heart that longed to do only what God wanted me to do. I wanted forgiveness for what I had done and to be put back into His good graces. My true desire was to get closer to God. I prayed David's prayer. "Let my passion for life be restored, tasting joy in every breakthrough You bring to me. Hold me close to You with a willing spirit that obeys whatever You say" (Psalms 51:12 TPT).

Breaking the stronghold I had allowed sugar to have over my life didn't happen all at once. I finally committed to work with God for the rest of my life to change my old habits and cultivate new ones.

SURRENDER

Surrendering to God was my next step. I thought I had done that years ago, but God convicted me that I was selfishly holding on to the kinds of foods I loved. It was time to let them go. It was time to completely surrender my fleshly desires to Him. Those were easy to identify. They were anything made with sugar and flour.

CHAPTER 16

Paul laid out what I needed to do in Romans 12:1 NIV. "I urge you, brothers and sisters, in view of God's mercy, to offer your bodies as a living sacrifice, holy and pleasing to God—this is your true and proper worship."

The Message says it this way. "So, here's what I want you to do, God helping you: Take your everyday, ordinary life—your sleeping, eating, going-to-work, and walking-around life—and place it before God as an offering." This throws food issues into the mix. I was OK with the rest of the things, but I knew I had not given the foods I loved to God as an offering.

What would it look like for me to surrender sugar to God? Could I even do that? No diet had ever told me I had to stop eating sugar for the rest of my life. It felt truly impossible, even improbable to me. However, the more I looked back over my life the more I knew it was something I had to do.

RICH YOUNG RULER WENT AWAY SAD

Then, God reminded me of the story of the rich, young ruler. He asked Jesus how to have eternal life. He said he'd followed all the rules. Jesus told him to sell everything and give the money to the poor.

The man couldn't give up what meant the most to him and went away sad because he had a lot of money. The disciples asked then who in the world can be saved? Jesus said, "What is impossible for people is possible with God" (Luke 18:27 NLT).

If the man had trusted God with his wealth, then he would be saved. This was impossible for him to do because he was counting on his money to get him through life. I realized I had been counting on the foods I loved to get me through life. I had to surrender those to God. I had to change my habits.

I was ready. Thankfully, my mentor was a tremendous help with this process. I learned that I couldn't sustain a diet on my own, but I could change my habits one at a time and step into a freedom I never knew existed.

HABIT CHANGE IS A JOURNEY

I had surrendered sugar to God, but I knew I couldn't stop eating it all at once because I would just start eating it again. It had to be a slow, gradual, but all-encompassing change for me.

Fitness instructor Jillian Michaels says it this way: "Transformation is not five minutes from now; it's a present activity. In this moment you can make a different choice. It's these small choices and successes that build up over time to help cultivate a healthy self-image and self-esteem."

What I learned on my habit-change journey is a stop without a start is just a diet. We will go back to the way we've always eaten if we don't start a new, better habit in its place. This is why diets don't work, but lifestyle change does. It brings new habits into our lives, which if we continue to do them regularly, will override the old habits we have formed.

A habit is a short-cut we have programmed into our brains by doing it over and over to get a specific reward or feeling. We do it on autopilot. We don't stop and think about it. To change a bad habit, we have to put a new, better habit in its place that will give us the same kind of reward. It may take two to three weeks of intentionally stopping the bad habit and putting a good habit in its place to override the old habit.

I started with my trigger food, which was candy. I decided to stop eating candy and start exercising three times a week for 30 minutes. It was amazing. Exercise made me feel so much

CHAPTER 16

better than eating candy did. So much so, that I looked forward to exercise and threw the candy away. After making exercise a new habit, I began stopping other bad habits and starting good ones in their place, one stop-start at a time.

STOP A BAD HABIT, START A GOOD ONE

It takes time to do this, but it was highly successful for me. For 30 years I had been trying to diet and all that happened was gaining weight instead of losing it. In light of that, habit change looks like a blip on the timeline of my life. It's the key that helped me lose 250 pounds and keep it off.

God showed me a verse in Galatians in a different light than I had ever seen it. It says: "Let us not grow weary of doing good, for in due season we will reap if we do not give up" (Galatians 6:9 ESV). I never thought of this verse in regard to taking care of myself, but it really fits in that context. We give up on ourselves way too soon.

I admire those in my coaching group who have stayed with the process and didn't give up even though they had setbacks. The great thing about a group is that there are others on the journey with you, who have the same issues and yet, encourage you to keep going.

He wants us to get so close to Jesus that we develop the mind of Christ. He wants to help us, but He can't help us if we are fighting against Him. "Whenever someone turns to the Lord, the veil is taken away. For the Lord is the Spirit, and wherever the Spirit of the Lord is, there is freedom" (II Corinthians 3:16-17 NLT).

God wants to transform us into His image. "All of us who have had that veil removed can see and reflect the glory of the

Lord. And the Lord—who is the Spirit—makes us more and more like Him as we are changed into His glorious image" (II Corinthians 3:18 NLT).

Transformation or change is what God desires for us. This is why a simple, man-made plan won't work. We need God's leadership every step of our transformation journey.

Our goal should not just be to lose weight. Our goal should be to transform into the person God desires us to be. That means we must follow Him. We must listen to Him. We must do what He says. This is a lot more difficult than just following a diet plan. It encompasses every part of us—spirit, soul and body.

I used to think the only part of me that was out of kilter was my body. Now I know that was not true. We are complex beings. If one part of us seems greatly out of sync, then every part of us is out of alignment.

> Our goal should be to transform into the person God wants us to be, not just to lose weight.

The most important part of us is our spirit. If our spirit is in line with God's Spirit, if we are listening to Him, following His voice, and doing what He tells us to do, then our bodies will begin to fall in line as well.

We have to want to change, submit to God, repent of all we have done wrong, surrender what we love more than God to Him, and do what He tells us to do.

It's so simple and so difficult at the same time. Just remember, "With God all things are possible" (Matthew 19:26 NIV). You and God got this!

CHAPTER 16

PRAY THIS PRAYER

"Father God, more than anything else, I desire transformation. I want to lose weight, but more than that I want to follow You.

"I want to listen to You and do what You tell me to do. Please, make it clear and plain to me what that is.

"Help me renew my mind. Help me focus my spirit on following Your Holy Spirit. Help me to desire transformation over everything else.

"Help me to want to surrender to You the foods I love that are dragging me down, causing me pain, and making me gain weight.

"I surrender them to You, right now.

"In Jesus' name. Amen."

ANSWER THESE QUESTIONS

1. List all the diets you've been on.

2. In what ways have these diets worked and not worked for you?

3. Why do you want to lose weight?

4. How willing are you to learn a different way other than a diet to lose weight and keep it off?

5. How does the story of the rich, young ruler relate to you and your reluctance to give up the foods you love?

6. Is physical transformation your only goal or are you open to spiritual transformation that can lead to physical change? What can you do to implement spiritual transformation?

CHAPTER 16

7. Are you willing to let God reveal to you how to let go of the lifestyle of the old self-life and be made new by every revelation that has been given to you? Are you ready, really ready, to be transformed and embrace your new life? Ask God how you can do that and write what He tells you.

CHAPTER 17

GOD DOESN'T CARE IF I AM FAT

God doesn't care if I am fat. He wants me to enjoy my life. He wants me to live, love, and be happy. Food makes me happy so I'm just doing what He wants me to do. There are things in this excuse which are true and things which are false.

This is true of every excuse. It's why we make excuses to begin with. They are pretty little lies filled with partial truths that make us think we are doing the right things when we aren't.

While it is true God really doesn't look on our outward appearance, He does care about our health. When I weighed over 430 pounds God still loved me, but He was very concerned about me. He knew I was unhealthy and going downhill fast.

Many I know in my family and among friends have died of heart issues. A heart issue was the thing that caused the cardiac surgeon to stamp an expiration date on my body and that hurt really badly. He gave me five years to live if I didn't lose weight and keep it off.

CHAPTER 17

That's the bad news. The good news is that was 23 years ago. By changing what I ate and still eat, I extended my life by 18 years and counting.

God never told me I was fat, even when I was super morbidly obese .He always spoke to me in kind and loving ways. However, don't tell me God doesn't care if I am fat. My appearance in no way affects His love for me. However, if someone is super morbidly obese like I was, He does care. He wants us to be healthy. If we are Christians, His Holy Spirit lives inside of us. Our bodies are His temple, His dwelling place, His home.

When God sees us, He sees the potential for our lives to bring Him glory. He also sees the real possibility for us to ruin our potential. I was doing a really good job of that. I'm not talking about a small amount of weight I had to lose. I'm talking about over 250 pounds I needed to lose. It was too great of a number for me to even think about.

SMALL SUCCESSES ARE GREAT MOTIVATORS

Recently an Overcomers Academy member asked me, if when I started my transformation journey did I have a specific amount of pounds I wanted to lose? My answer was, "I just wanted to lose the next pound. Any more was too much for me to think about." Since I lost the weight over a span of about nine years, I really didn't think about the total amount of weight I lost until God asked me to write my memoir, *Sweet Grace*.

Then I counted up my weight loss and was totally surprised to realize from the highest weight I reached to where I was right then was 250 pounds. I had weighed 430 pounds when I was in the hospital, but I know I weighed more than that at one time. I had gotten to the point where I couldn't weigh even on a 500-pound scale. When you are that large, you don't want to know what you weigh.

Focusing on the next pound I needed to lose was all I could do. Small successes are great motivators. I counted every small success. Every pound counted. Every clothing size I went down counted. Every time I cleaned out my closet and put my fat clothes in the garage counted. Every time I passed up dessert even though I longed for it counted.

I was finally on God's side, which was really my side. I just hadn't seen it that way. He wanted me to stop eating foods made with sugar and flour because He knew they were killing me. More than that, He wanted me to lose that monstrous amount of weight and not be afraid to write and speak about it. He wants to use me to bring hope to you and enable you to move these truths down deep inside your own heart and apply them to your lives. God wants you to be healthy because He has a purpose for your life. He does!

> I had to learn how to stop craving the foods I loved and learn how to start craving God.

I thought eating sugary junk foods made me happy, but I discovered I was not happy. My body was way too large. This made me very unhappy. It made me stay at a distance from people. Who wants a big, fat lady hugging them. They might think my fat was contagious.

In order to really live, love, and be happy I had to learn how to stop craving the foods I loved and learn how to start craving God. We can crave things that are bad for us or we

CHAPTER 17

can crave what is good for us. We can stop craving the bad things and start craving the good things. Let those words soak into your heart and soul because it is where true happiness is found. To do this we must allow the Holy Spirit to direct us. This is important not just in weight loss but in our direction and purpose as we walk through this lie.

The apostle John explained, "This world is fading away, along with everything that people crave. But anyone who does what pleases God will live forever" (I John 1:17 NLT).

Peter said, "Like newborn babies, crave pure spiritual milk, so that by it you may grow up in your salvation, now that you have tasted that the Lord is good" (I Peter 2:2-3 NIV). We must crave God and not the things that will put us in early graves.

FILLED WITH GOD'S JOY

God wants us to be filled with joy, His joy. Happy is a momentary thing. Happy is what we think we feel when we take that first bite of cake. Misery is what comes when we realize we've eaten half the cake and could eat the rest if we were sure no one else would notice.

Joy is what comes when God fulfills our longings. Joy is His strength coursing through us to give us the power to overcome temptation. True joy is a limitless, life-defining, transformative reservoir waiting to be tapped into. It requires the utmost surrender and, like love, it is a choice.

Joy is a choice we can make, but first it requires surrender. We must surrender what we think is making us feel good in the moment but is not in reality giving us lasting joy. Any substance we think we can't live without will put us in bondage until we realize Jesus is the only one who can set us free and keep us free when we follow Him.

Lasting joy can only be found when we follow the Holy Spirit's leading in all that we do. Remember the Proverbs 31 woman? She was an excellent wife, mother, entrepreneur, home manager, and boss.

CLOTHED WITH STRENGTH AND DIGNITY

Here's what we need to remember about her. "She is clothed with strength and dignity; she can laugh at the days to come" (Proverbs 31:25 NIV). Laughter is momentary, but I get the picture of this excellent woman having joy in everything she does so much so that laughter just comes naturally to her.

It doesn't come from the food she eats, though she manages her household well and they have enough to eat. It comes from her dedication to God. That is outlined in these verses. "Many women do noble things, but you surpass them all. Charm is deceptive, and beauty is fleeting; but a woman who fears the Lord is to be praised" (Proverbs 31:29-30 NIV).

This woman is not being praised solely because of her looks, her charm, her size, her industrious work for her family, what she eats, or what she cooks. It is because she fears the Lord. It is because she follows what He wants her to do and not only what she wants.

The Passion Translation says it this way, "Charm can be misleading, and beauty is vain and so quickly fades, but this virtuous woman lives in the wonder, awe, and fear of the Lord. She will be praised throughout eternity" (Proverbs 31:30 TPT). That's my desire and I imagine it is yours as well.

CHAPTER 17

What is it that God really wants for us? He doesn't want us to chow down on every food that makes us momentarily happy. God wants us to understand we first have to settle who we are. If we don't know our identity, we can't know the purpose He has for our lives. Here are six things God has waiting for us if we choose to take advantage of them.

SIX THINGS GOD WANTS FOR US

First, if we have accepted Christ as our Savior, we are in Him. "Because of Him you are in Christ Jesus, who became to us wisdom from God, righteousness and sanctification and redemption" (I Corinthians 1:30 ESV). If we are in Christ, we cannot be taken out of Him. He is the one who shares God's wisdom with us. He keeps us on track.

Second, if we are His, we are members of the body of Christ. "Now you are the body of Christ and individually members of it" (I Corinthians 6:17 ESV). That means we are representatives of Christ here on earth. Are we representing Him well? Are we doing what He wants us to do?

Third, because we are in Christ and a member of the body of Christ, we have become one with Him. This is a big deal. It means whatever we do reflects directly on Jesus. "He who is joined to the Lord becomes one spirit with Him" (I Corinthians 6:17 NIV).

Fourth, we are to be built up in Him. "So then, just as you received Christ Jesus as Lord, continue to live your lives in Him, rooted and built up in Him, strengthened in the faith as you were taught, and overflowing with thankfulness" (Colossians 2:6-7 ESV).

Fifth, we can't be concerned with things that are fleshly, carnal, sinful, and of this earth. We must set our minds on God and His Spirit. Our flesh has died. Those desires that are against what God wants for us have to go. Our lives should be hidden with Christ in God. That means our desires should be the same as God's desires for us. "Set your minds on things that are above, not on things that are on earth. For you have died, and your life is hidden with Christ in God" (Colossians 3:2-3 ESV).

Sixth, we must surrender our desires to God. Without handing those things to God, they will become more important to us than God. Jesus told us this in no uncertain terms. "Do not lay up for yourselves treasures on earth, where moth and rust destroy and where thieves break in and steal, but lay up for yourselves treasures in heaven, where neither moth nor rust destroys and where thieves do not break in and steal. For where your treasure is, there your heart will be also" (Matthew 6:19-21 ESV).

If we don't surrender to God, we will find ourselves surrendering to something that will wreak havoc in our lives. There are so many things on this earth that can take us under: money, sex, food, drugs, pornography, alcohol, job security, retirement funds, bigger house, newer car, fame, and glory. That's just to name a few.

WHAT IS SATISFACTION?

Only following God will satisfy our deepest cravings for belonging. Not fame. Not excitement. Not glory. Not suff. Not money. Not food. We must give God anything we have allowed to be more important than Him.

CHAPTER 17

Control over our desires is an issue many of us have. We protect our desires at all costs. However, if the thing we're trying to control is we get to eat what we want when we want it, that means we have an issue with food. Whatever things we are trying to hang on to for some reason and feel we can't hand to God are what has become our god. They will not satisfy us. As a food and sugar addict, I have learned the safest thing I can do is hand those foods I desire to God.

He alone knows me because He alone made me. Why would I refuse to trust Him with all the things that are difficult on my journey? "But now, O Lord, You are our Father; we are the clay, and You are our potter; we are all the work of Your hand" (Isaiah 64:8 ESV).

> God tells us the most beautiful and earth-shattering thing. He says simply, "I love you."

God gives us promises that we can hang our hats on. "But now thus says the Lord, He who created you, O Jacob, He who formed you, O Israel: 'Fear not, for I have redeemed you; I have called you by name, you are Mine. When you pass through the waters, I will be with you; and through the rivers, they shall not overwhelm you; when you walk through fire you shall not be burned, and the flame shall not consume you" (Isaiah 43:1-2 ESV).

Any promise from the Old Testament that mentions Israel is a promise for us if we believe in Christ because we have been grafted into Him. In verses three and four He continued to tell us that He is the Lord our God, our Savior, and we are precious and honored in His eyes.

Then right there at the end of verse four, He tells us the most beautiful and earth-shattering thing of all, the thing that should make us want to surrender completely to Him and follow Him all of our days. He says simply, "I love you" (Isaiah 43:4 ESV). Wait! Did God, the God of the universe, just say that He is madly in love with me no matter what I have or haven't done? He most certainly did.

I can submit to a God like that. I can surrender the things I desire for what He knows will fulfill my longings. I can do that because I know He loves me and knows me better than I know myself. The same is true for you. He loves you. He really, really loves you.

It's time to show Him that you love Him, as well. The only way to do that is to surrender the things you crave to Him, trust Him to lead you, and then follow Him.

PRAY THIS PRAYER

"Dear Jesus, thank You for loving me. Thank You for dying on the cross for me.

"Thank You for leading me. Thank You for continually convicting me when my cravings are greater than my love for You.

"I want to show you that I love You, too.

"Right now, I surrender my cravings and desires to You.

"I exchange those things that are weighing me down for the wonderful things You have promised when I simply follow You.

"I'm ready. Lead me, Lord. I will follow.

"In Jesus' name. Amen."

CHAPTER 17

ANSWER THESE QUESTIONS

1. What has God done for you? What does He want you to do for Him? If you don't know, ask Him.

2. Read Matthew 6:19-21 ESV. What or who has my heart? Give evidence of that from your life.

3. Is there something you desire more than you desire God? What is it? Why have you put it above God in your life?

4. If God told you to give it up, could you? Why or why not? And when will you stop making that excuse?

5. What will bring you lasting joy? How is that different from happiness?

6. Read Isaiah 43:4 ESV. How can you return God's love?

7. Take some time right now to list the things you know you need to hand to God. Write them on small pieces of paper. Then when you are ready, one at a time hand them to God and prayerfully ask Him what do you give me in exchange? what He gives you will be one of His treasures. Write that down. Keep that list. Now tear up or burn each thing you handed to God as a symbolic gesture of Him taking your ashes and giving you back the beauty or the treasure He wants you to have.

CHAPTER 17

*"This world
is fading way,
along with everything
that people crave.
But anyone
who does what
pleases God
will live forever!"*

1 JOHN 1:17 NLT

NEXT STEPS

I have been a master at excuses. Excuses kept me from God's best for way too long. My hope is that God turned on some lightbulbs for you as you read this book.

If you are stuck in an excuse, the great thing is you don't have to stay stuck. I have more resources to help. On my website, you can access my coaching group, one-on-one coaching, podcast episodes, blogs, and books. There are free resources, as well.

By far, my best resource is Overcomers Christian Weight Loss Coaching Academy. In Overcomers Academy, we have a guided experience through my extensive video course library. We also have monthly live video calls, weekly encouragement room calls, and a private Facebook group for connection. The information and signup page for this and one-on-one coaching is on my website under the weight loss tab.

THE CHAPTER I LEFT OUT

Over on my website, you can find the chapter I left out of this book. It's called *Why God Hates Excuses*. You can find it under the free tab on my website.

It's a great way to introduce the content of this book to others and you'll find some advice there, as well.

The url for the free chapter is: https://TeresaShieldsParker.com/why-God-hates-excuses/.

I designed *Sweet Excuses* to use for your personal study. However, it is also perfect to use for a small group study or a book club discussion group. Just use the questions at the end of each chapter to encourage each other and stimulate discussion.

If you do study this book in a group, please drop me an email or find me on social media and let me know. I love to hear how people are using my books.

As always, I'd love to connect with you on any of my social media channels. You can find them on the next page. I do enjoy hearing from you. Feel free to contact me by email with questions or insights. You can find me everywhere.

PLEASE WRITE A REVIEW

One other thing, every author probably tells you this, but it would be very helpful if you would write a review of *Sweet Excuses* and share it on Amazon where you find this book.

People read the reviews to help them decide whether or not they want to read the book. I am convinced that this book can jumpstart many to follow God more closely and step out of food bondage for the rest of their lives.

That's my purpose in a nutshell. I actually voice it this way, "I teach women how to work with God to transform their lives, lose weight, and live healthy." Everything I do is focused there from my books, to podcast, blog posts, and coaching.

I'm thanking you in advance for writing a review and checking out other resources I have that may help you. You rock!

NEXT STEPS

LET'S CONNECT

Website: https://TeresaShieldsParker.com

Emil: Info@TeresaShieldsParker.com

Amazon: https://amazon.com/author/teresashieldsparker/

Podcast: https://TeresaShieldsParker.com/Podcast/

Youtube: https://youtube.com/teresashieldsparker1/

Facebook: https://www.facebook.com/TeresaShieldsParker

Instagram: https://www.instagram.com/treeparker/

Pinterest: https://www.pinterest.com/treeparker/

Group: https://TeresaShieldsParker.com/overcomers/

One-on-One Coaching:

https://TeresaShieldsParker.com/one-on-one-freedom-coaching

SWEET GRACE

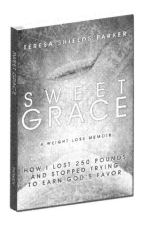

Sweet Grace: How I Lost 250 Pounds and Stopped Trying to Earn God's Favor is a tell-all memoir about my loss journey. My first book, it is the most widely read. She tells her story with honesty and transparency. *Sweet Grace Study Guide* is also available on Amazon. It includes a chapter-by-chapter study, along with additional resources.

SWEET CHANGE

Sweet Change: True Stories of Transformation includes stories of 17 people who have lost weight. They discuss their moments of change. I give some insight and advice about the change process in order to help readers discover their personal motivation for beginning a transformation journey. It is available on Amazon.

SWEET FREEDOM

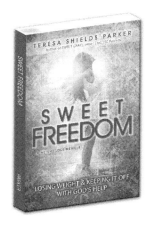

Sweet Freedom: Losing Weight and Keeping it Off includes how to deal with core issues that keep us stuck. The walls will crumble when we are willing to dig deep and work with God for our answers. Separate *Sweet Freedom Study Guide* includes principles section and step-by-step action steps and activities for each chapter. Both books are available on Amazon.

NEXT STEPS

SWEET SURRENDER

Sweet Surrender: Breaking Strongholds addresses life-controlling problems, such as addictions of all kinds and issues with relationships, shame, vocational direction, emotional issues, fear, weight, and more. Strongholds keep us stuck. God wants to help us break free so we can live out the destiny and plans He has for us. Includes questions and action steps for each chapter. Available on Amazon.

SWEET JOURNEY

Sweet Journey to Transformation: Practical Steps to Lose Weight and Live Healthy is the book I wrote after dissecting my journey. It includes the five stages of weight loss and steps within each stage which help us move towards becoming overcomers. These steps are how I lost 250 pounds. Study guide for each chapter included. It is available on Amazon.

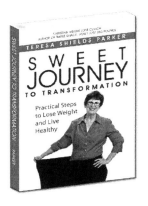

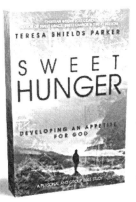

SWEET HUNGER

Sweet Hunger: Developing an Appetite for God is a Bible study exploring the importance of craving God more than our favorite foods. It examines eight Bible stories where food is a central issue. I share the connection between God's truth He presents in each story. Includes questions and activities for each chapter. A video teaching can be purchased and downloaded from my website. Book available on Amazon.

ABOUT THE AUTHOR

Teresa Shields Parker is an author, coach, podcaster, and speaker who has lost 250 pounds and has kept it off for going on 10 years.

She is the author of the number one Christian Weight Loss memoir, Sweet Grace: How I Lost 250 Pounds and Stopped Trying to Earn God's Favor. Sweet Excuses is her seventh book.

She resides in Columbia, MO with her husband of 45 years and two beautiful Birman cats. She loves to write, paint, do water exercise, and hang out with friends and family.

Made in the USA
Columbia, SC
17 December 2024

49767016R00141